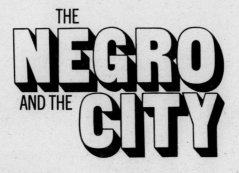

THE NEGRO AND THE CITY

THE

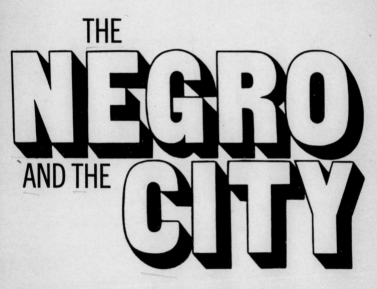

NEGRO

AND THE CITY

ADAPTED FROM A SPECIAL ISSUE OF FORTUNE ON:
"BUSINESS AND THE URBAN CRISIS"

TIME-LIFE BOOKS, NEW YORK

TABLE OF CONTENTS

N 106

PREFACE

One night in July, 1967, James M. Roche, then the president (and later the chairman) of General Motors Corp., was working late on the fourteenth floor of the G.M. Building in Detroit. As he was mulling over the affairs of his enormously complex corporation he was disturbed by an eerie flickering. He looked out to see his city in flames—"I never thought I would see anything like that." Since then, with a group of fellow Detroiters of equal stature, Roche has made "the city" his most urgent business.

By some standards, the conversion of corporate America to the cause of the cities is woefully late. Still, it comes at the time when it is most needed. Those traditional custodians of cities, the politicians, the officeholders, the welfare workers, the federal grants-in-aid men, and even the academic consultants, are recoiling in dismay at their collective failure—although, as the first chapter of this book indicates, the failure lies more broadly on us all.

The best effort of American business is indispensable in the urban crisis. This is not a parochial conclusion. It is, rather, the net of confidences volunteered by people in virtually all ranks of government, from Cabinet level to the embattled precinct station. And the business potential is impressive.

This book, adapted from the January, 1968, issue of FORTUNE, is dedicated to the proposition that American business can lead the way to a better urban society. But the frame of mind of some ten million urban Negroes (page 41) is evidence enough that optimism is premature.

LOUIS BANKS
MANAGING EDITOR, FORTUNE

INTRODUCTION

This book is an excellent statement on—and a pleading for—leadership by American business in the fight for a better urban society.

It deserves reading by all who have parts to play in the urban crisis, for it eloquently describes the main stumbling block faced—a common apathy, much of it rooted in myths we have inherited.

Apathy at the poverty level is well known, born out of hopelessness and frustration. This frustration erupts from time to time in mob violence in the streets—and some can see a form of hope for the future in such outbursts. But no one can find cause for hope in the day-after-day apathy that grips the great majority of the poor.

There is another widespread apathy, less known but equally wasteful and tragic for America. This is the apathy of well-to-do and middle-income people toward our complex urban problems. One hears it rationalized many ways: "The poor could work if they wanted to"; "Somehow things always work out"; "Private business must concentrate on profits"; "Cities are beyond saving, even if they are worth saving."

As Max Ways shows in his outstanding article on "The Deeper Shame of Our Cities," business has been one of the chief victims of the dominant American social myth that cities are to be despised. This myth from our agrarian past included contempt for the big businesses of the cities as well as for the slum poor. And the contempt lingers to this day.

But many corporate officials are shaking off the yoke of apathy. Recent events have baffled and frightened some; others have learned that their companies have goals in common with those of the cities and the Negroes in the ghettos. In the process, businessmen are committing themselves to the problems of our cities. They are utilizing their unique talents, experience, and skills in an effort to help the poor help themselves. And as they do this, they act as responsible citizens and neighbors, as well as efficient merchants and producers.

The problems ahead require not only participation by diverse groups but also a better understanding between them. Closer working relationships between management and labor, for example, will undoubtedly develop as a result of their mutual interest in rebuilding urban America. As the partnership matures, labor will come to recognize the new role of business on the urban scene, and business will appreciate the contributions of organized labor to improvement of urban life and realization of civil rights. Together they will offer greater employment opportunities for the urban poor.

It is well to understand that, if we are to meet the urban crisis, we must think less in terms of who leads and more in terms of who joins the team. In our Model Cities Program, we require exactly this sort of group effort, a joining of hands by all concerned—businessmen, urban specialists, union and church leaders, civic groups, state and local officials, and, not last or least or on a token basis, the residents of the slums themselves.

> ROBERT C. WEAVER,
> *Secretary of Housing and Urban Development*

1

THE DEEPER SHAME OF THE CITIES

by Max Ways

> *"If you got the big red apple, man,*
> *you got the worm, too."*

Along with American success there has always been the recurrent pain, the spasms of self-doubt, of fear, of desperate conflict. Most versions of our history are glossily cheerful, but in truth, as an American once told Jacques Maritain, "We are bruised souls." Real risk of failure, of collapse, has been present in every U.S. crisis: 1776, 1789, 1828, 1861, in the long traumatic uprootings of industrialization and mass immigration, and after that in 1917, 1932, and 1941. England was once called "merrie" and France "gay"; at no time have such lightsome adjectives been applied to the United States.

A nation that has often lived dangerously now stands again at the volcano's rim. At a time of our highest material success and at its symbolic center, Detroit, the 1967 riots poured out lava of hatred and destruction—and similar eruptions shook scores of other cities and towns. The pressures of racial tension that generated almost suicidal behavior, white and black, have not yet abated and will not abate of their own accord. For years ahead the most urgent internal business will be to contain and reduce these pressures. It would be reckless to underestimate our danger, to assume that because we have mastered other crises we will master this one. But it would be just as disastrous to assume that there is no possibility that we can restore our essential social unity.

The U.S., however, will not surmount the racial crisis unless it makes rapid progress toward resolving a broader, though less acute, crisis—that of "the city." In this context, "the city" means not just the great core cities of our metropolitan areas; it refers to the whole situs of contemporary American civilization, the nationwide complex, including satellite cities, suburbs, and towns. This has become one vast pulsing organism. Although many of its internal communications are awry and its organs badly coordinated one with another, our society is more interdependent than ever before and more so than any other society, past or present. Cut into thousands of political fragments ranging from great states to tiny villages, this whole subfederal level has had to cope with huge new burdens created by shifts of population and changes in the style of life. During the last thirty-five years, when public discussion concentrated mainly on Washington and on international affairs, the neglected subfederal level of our public life has been falling further and further behind the responsibilities thrust upon it by social change.

As it happens, most of the instruments by which society might deal with the Negro crisis (police, education, welfare, public health, and housing) are administered—and must continue to be administered—mainly at subfederal levels. The race crisis has pressed hardest at precisely those points where U.S. society's ability to cope was already weakest. This was made terrifyingly plain in the 1967 riots when, in city after city and town after town, police were unable to maintain order. The failure was predictable. Why expect effective riot control from the same law-enforcement apparatus that for fifty years has failed to break up organized crime, failed to contain the narcotics traffic, failed to protect citizens on the streets, failed to reform juvenile delinquents, failed even in traffic control and highway safety? A Negro leader walked into the office of a New York business executive and asked a good question: "How can a city which is not able to perform the simple job of getting the garbage off the streets hope to handle the really difficult problems of race relations?"

Trust is the cornerstone of civic order, but few of us, white or black, really trust the communities in which we live. We have no reason to suppose that they will keep the air and the rivers clean or that they can effectively protect our lives or our property. Expensive locks and burglar alarms multiply. The sale of firearms to private citizens has been mounting, especially since 1967's summer of riots—an ominous sign that men of both races have diminished confidence in the public authority's ability to keep the civil peace. Running away from the challenges of the city, we have let our communal competence decline and our civic trust drain away.

All this is no secret. The whole world knows the condition of U.S. cities—and has known it for decades. The billions we have poured out for foreign aid and propaganda, the more numerous billions we spend for military support of our foreign policy, are half-canceled by the damage that is done to U.S. prestige by our long-standing inability to deal effectively with gangsterism, slums, high infant death rates among our poor, traffic jams, junkyards, billboards, and all the rest of the noxious mess. What, much of the world asks, is the point of being the richest and most powerful nation, if such problems can't be handled better? What is the point of capitalism? Of democracy? And never forget that 95 percent of what's

wrong with the city developed before the crisis in race relations. "The Negro problem" represents a crisis within a
crisis, a specific and acute syndrome in a body already ill
from more general disorders.

Just as every past agony of U.S. history resulted in a deepening of the American experience and a strengthening of the
American Proposition about human freedom, so the Negro crisis, by pressing hard upon the long-standing defects of U.S.
communities, can make us understand how much is unnec-
essarily faulty in American life, white as well as black. For
instance, we now begin to understand that much more than
formal "equality" is needed to make the school system effective for the children of the Negro poor. Now we can see
how special government and corporation educational programs, using methods different from those of the school
system, are producing astonishingly good results among Negro dropouts. Thus we acquire a comparative basis for judging
how inflexible, unimaginative, unenterprising, and ineffective
our bureaucratically ossified school system, *in toto,* has become. The drive for substantial improvement of Negro
education may show us how to construct, for all children, a
far better school system than the one we now have. To take
another example, the Job Corps, assigned to make employ-
ables out of unemployable youngsters, found that 80 percent
of its applicants had not seen a doctor or dentist for ten
years. This tells us something about the health condition of
the poor. It also provides a clue to a more general, if less obvious, defect in U.S. society: the organizational weakness of its
medical services, which for over twenty years failed to react
to the plainly predictable shortage of doctors and nurses
that is now upon us.

Atlanta has had for many years a far more vigorous and forward-looking leadership than most U.S. cities. Even so, Atlanta today is not making much progress with such problems as mounting racial segregation within city neighborhoods, overburdened schools in Negro areas, and the flight of middle-income whites to surrounding counties—an exodus that, of course, severely limits the central city's ability to provide adequate services for its resident population. It is interesting to note that on simpler problems, not specifically connected with race, Atlanta is in grave trouble. For instance, the relatively new Northeast Expressway links Atlanta with DeKalb County, whose well-to-do population has grown in twenty-seven years from 87,000 to 360,000. Between 7:00 and 9:00 a.m. and between 4:00 and 6:00 p.m. expressway traffic creeps, fume-hung and thwarted. Its Brookwood interchange, built to take a maximum of 52,500 cars a day, is now burdened with 122,000 cars. No doubt, a suburban resident who has to spend hours on that road is still better off than Negroes living along an unpaved street of Atlanta's Summerhill district. But the failure of Atlanta to solve its transportation problems gives a large part of the answer as to why that city—along with many others—is grinding toward a halt in its sincere efforts to ameliorate its racial conflicts.

The nationwide sluggishness and ineptitude in dealing with change does not apply only to government agencies. The universities and the whole intellectual community have not been much interested in the problems of the city. American business, busily generating change, has in the main stood apart from the responsibilities—and the opportunities—of coping with the community needs that arise from change. Since mid-year of 1967, and largely as a response to the race crisis, this business attitude toward the problems of the city is shifting. The ardent efforts of the nation's business institutions will be especially needed, because they have qualities demanded by the double crisis of the Negro and the city. Modern corporations are flexible and innovative. They are accustomed to sensing and meeting and evoking the changing desires of the public. Above all, they practice the difficult art of mobilizing specialized knowledge for action—i.e., the art of managing change.

As the U.S. begins to apply its immense public and private resources to creating the future of the city, it should remember to keep the two crises in perspective. The Negro protest has performed the service of awakening us to our society's weakness. And we cannot deal with Negro unrest without remedying social defects that extend far beyond the Negro problem. In short, the U.S. cannot be made fit for the black man unless it is also made fit for the white man.

This word "fit" implies a criterion that is not self-evident. The U.S., from time to time in the past, has been fit, in the sense of not deeply and obviously disturbed. The state of the nation has not declined in any way that can be measured on scales of quantity. Materially, all groups, even the vast majority of Negroes, have much more than their grandfathers and fathers had. U.S. Negroes in the aggregate have income and educational levels about the same as the population of Great Britain. By what standard, then, can the level of U.S. life, black or white, be judged inadequate, unfit?

Another element must be inserted into the criterion, an element very hard to measure or define. In most of the world there is a spreading, deepening sense that individuals, communities, and nations have much more ability to get things done than they used to have. This ability to move toward where we want to go—or ought to go—is called "power," which, in all its conjunct and disjunct forms (technological, organizational, communicatory), is increasing everywhere. The statement that the U.S. is unfit implies a judgment that we are failing in the sense that we now have the capability of making this nation a much better place to live in than it is. The idea that power is rising expands the idea of duty, or responsibility. Nobody can be blamed, or blame himself, for not doing what he can't; when he can and doesn't, unrest, internal conflict, and shame may result.

Referring usually to underdeveloped countries, this new kind of unrest is called "the revolution of rising expectations." In case after case the expectations, individual and national, outrun any practical possibility that enough power can be applied to satisfy them in the near future. This overexpectation is not universal. One finds around the world many examples of peoples accepting, in one or another area of their lives, unfavorable conditions, material and immaterial, that would seem quite possible of correction. "Low expectations" can be said to characterize the British standard of an acceptable economic growth rate, the Russian standard of an acceptable level of civil liberties or consumer goods, or the standard that Ireland accepts about how old a man should be to marry.

The double crisis in the U.S. can be seen as a rear-end collision in which accelerating Negro expectations have rammed into the sluggish tendency of American whites to demand too little of the quality of city life and to appraise too humbly the quality of citizenship that the city of the future should demand of them. Many Negroes are now insisting upon faster progress than it may be possible for the U.S. to deliver under optimum circumstances—even assuming a rapid regeneration of the city. Until the 1950's, U.S. Negroes were as a group characterized by very low expectations and an even lower assessment of the power they might be able to exercise within the nation. After the 1954 Supreme Court decision in *Brown v. Board of Education* touched off a campaign to enforce school desegregation, Negro demands on society began to rise very rapidly. Martin Luther King's Montgomery bus boycott in 1956 was an early example of the successful application of power. In the Sixties, Negroes had further experience of political power in the passage of civil-rights laws stronger than most observers had believed possible.

In ten years U.S. Negroes were transformed from an apathetic group, hard to organize or stir, to a position of extreme discontent and militancy that characterizes the modern world's high expectation peoples. But when Negroes turned from such mainly symbolic goals as civil-rights legislation to the hard practicalities that could be won only at the level of the city, they began to experience intense frustration culminating in the 1967 riots. Not for the first time in history, a group that had been peacefully apathetic in extremely adverse circumstances turned rebellious after it had begun to feel its power and after some of its worst grievances were on the way to redress.

Television played a large part in this amazing upsurge of the Negro's demands. Into his living room was projected the white man's living room, the white man's glamorized life. Into the Negro's ears and eyes the TV commercials beat their insistent message of more, better, greater. In one sense, this was constructive—the old American warning against the acceptance of things as they are. Negroes wanted to participate—and not merely as "viewers" in this exciting and powerful society that surrounded them. But as desire rose and was not soon requited, frustration rose, too. Conflict appeared on the Negro's television screen, most dramatically in the Birmingham riots of 1963. All over the U.S., Negroes saw Bull Connor's dogs;

more precisely, they *felt* Bull Connor's dogs. A white teacher in Long Island, who had many friends among Negro youngsters, remembers that in the days after the Birmingham riots hostility that he had never noticed before glared at him from the kids' eyes. Frustrated Negroes all over the nation were suddenly prepared to listen to messages of hate from Malcolm X and Stokely Carmichael.

The resulting situation, the one the U.S. is now seized with, has been called "revolutionary"—not a word to be tossed around lightly. By itself, the rebellious mood of many Negroes would not constitute a revolutionary danger in a strong society that ought to be able to deal with such a thrust by some combination of concession and repression. But all truly revolutionary situations are marked by paralysis above as well as by insurrection below. The term "Negro revolution" must be taken seriously because its present battleground is at the level of the city, and at this level U.S. society has been half-paralyzed for decades. The 1967 riots were a warning that the city may be so functionally weak and confused that it will neither be able to concede what Negroes justly demand nor to repress the unlawful tactics that spring from the frustration of such demands.

It will be useless to counsel Negroes to patience unless there is among whites a visibly rising impatience to improve our civilization. The city is functionally enfeebled for reasons that pertain mainly to white, not black, America. The dominant race, so enterprising in its individual and corporate pursuits and so proudly resolute in the deployment of its national power in space exploration and war, has neglected a level in between. American whites have been unwilling to mobilize their material, intellectual, and aesthetic resources to achieve better communities, better ways of living together.

Like all the low-expectation peoples, we are uneasily half-aware that we have the power—and, therefore, the duty—to achieve a better life, and our failure to act in civil affairs upon this gnawing intimation of our strength leaves us feeling guilty and insecure. It is this demoralized side of U.S. white society that the Negro, himself disordered by injustice and frustration, now confronts.

As Plato discovered, the state is the product of a state of mind, the political reflection of how a people views its own nature. Our state of mind contains a yawning discrepancy between what we are and what we pretend to be. Our public myth is too remote from our actual lives.

The U.S. in the twentieth century is an urban nation, not in some superficial sense of its population densities, but in the fundamental sense that it is made up of diverse people, pluralistic in belief and habit, who live by exchanging the products of very different and highly specialized skills. A high degree of interdependence among heterogeneous inhabitants is the key characteristic of the modern city—what sets it apart from the typical agrarian society where each family unit, approaching economic self-sufficiency, tends to work and to live in the same way as every other family unit. Even our farmers today are specialists—and in that fundamental sense share the urban characteristic of almost total interdependence with other farmers and with nonfarmers. Our actual lives are lived in huge organizations joined by intricate market networks and systems of transportation and communication—one vast, teeming, coast-to-coast bazaar.

But that is not how we think of ourselves. The dominant American social myth is still Thomas Jefferson's set of values and ideals, which assumes a loosely knit and lightly organized society of independent farmers. This vision was and is contemptuous of cities and of those who dwell therein. The American ethos applauds Cowley's verse: "God the first garden made, and the first city Cain." The American dream of beauty tends to seek the unpeopled tops of mountains or to linger on solitary, separated men brooding by Walden Pond, toiling in forest clearings.

The agrarian myth reinforced itself by becoming the selective standard by which Americans chose which parts of their total experience to cherish and enshrine in memory, which to repress and forget. In the nineteenth century two tremendous American efforts were more or less simultaneously carried out: the conquest of the continent by small farmers and the assimilation of masses of immigrants (and of rural Americans) by the cities. In terms of the American Proposition implicit in the Constitution—the Proposition that assumes its principles to be applicable to all men who choose to accept freedom and responsibility—the achievement of the cities was at least equal to that of the pioneers who so fearlessly braved the poison-ivied woods across the Shenandoah.

But our hero-selection apparatus decreed that the conquest of the wilderness should be the one great American epic, while the Americanization and urbanization of the peasant hordes should be regarded almost as a discreditable episode. As the nineteenth century neared its end, Frederick Jackson Turner was delivering, over and over again, his extravagant and influential homage to the pioneer, his lecture called *The Winning of the West,* while Lincoln Steffens was writing *The Shame of the Cities*. Though he excoriated the corrupt political machines, Steffens was perceptive enough to recognize how their warmth contributed to the assimilation of the strangers and the poor. ("Tammany kindness is real kindness, and will go far, remember long, and take infinite trouble for a friend.") But this constructive function of city machine politics was rejected by the all-powerful anti-urban bent of the American value system. When, in 1960, a Boston Irishman whose grandparents had been associated with one of those machines became the first true child of the city elected President of the United States, even he made his compulsory obeisance to the dominant agrarian myth by naming his Administration "the New Frontier."

Television, that great engine of mythology, is both the victim and the exploiter of frontiersmanship. Imagine the cries of anguish and outrage that would arise if TV presented to our children some dramas of the urban struggles and triumphs of the 1880's, including (as realism would require) a little indoor bribery and corruption. Respectable Americans would insist that children's TV continue to be monopolized by the winning of the West, where nothing more unedifying occurs than red-blooded American outdoor homicide.

For generations we were taught to despise our cities until they became, indeed, despicable. Their demoralization and decline hastened—and were hastened by—the flight of millions of Americans to the suburbs, in which each man can act out the agrarian fantasy by owning a minifarmhouse behind a minimeadow, where no mule grazes. In certain political and social arrangements, too, the suburbanites realized the agrarian daydream. These bedroom communities, though economically and culturally dependent on the core cities and on one another, adopted political forms of local government appropriate for isolated Vermont mountain villages a hundred years ago. In their social make-up, the suburbs increasingly reflected the agrarian ideal of homogeneity. Those developed before 1925 had a fairly wide range of lot size, price, and architectural style, and attracted a diverse population; that is to say, early suburbs were socially somewhat like cities. But decade by decade, suburbs become more sharply stratified as to income level, house style, and life style. ("We like to live with our own kind of people.") The peasant daydream obsessed the nation, which, in its actual life, was moving further and further from its peasant past.

Up until the 1920's, cities, towns, and suburbs had shown a healthy tendency to coalesce politically as their built-up areas came in contact with one another and as their economic interdependence increased. But then the trend toward annexation and consolidation slowed down, especially around the older cities. The fluidity of the city began to clot. Failure of political forms to follow the patterns of actual life indicated that some maleficent chemistry, some poison, was at work in the public mind. The stockade mentality—keep out the barbarians, "the others"—was curdling the idea of the city.

Fear of the Negro was not the precipitating agent of this change; it began before he was an important presence in most cities outside the South. Until quite recent years, the whites fleeing to suburbia were not running away from the Negro but from one another and from the challenges of urban life. But the triumph of suburbia and the anti-urban psychology that it represents have indeed become a major element in creating both the present Negro crisis and the crisis of the city. When millions of Negroes during and after World War II began flowing out of rural areas, the host cities were less capable of performing for them the assimilative function that had been successful decades ago for other ethnic groups. Racial bigotry was, of course, the most conspicuous element in this failure, but the deeper cause was a general anti-urban regression, which between 1900 and 1940 had affected the value system of white society and consequently weakened the vitality and the usefulness of its urban institutions.

In the nineteenth century the city had had a strong, though often unofficial and corrupt, government. When the backroom boys in the clubhouse said, "We've got to take care of Mike," they had in mind the whole range of Mike's problems of adjusting to American life—his illiteracy and incompetence, his wife's alcoholism, his kids' delinquency. Such help as the clubhouse could give was inexpert and performed at a heavy, though hidden, social cost by such devices as loading city and traction company payrolls with incompetent workers. Mike's life, uprooted by migration, was a bruising experience; nevertheless, Mike knew that in many ways the clubhouse— and, therefore, City Hall—was on his side, that it was aware of him in his whole humanity, and even that it was responsive to his preferences. From the day he got off the boat, Mike, in a way, belonged. A reciprocal awareness, a mutual trust, between Mike and what we would now call "the power structure" was crucial to the Americanization of Mike and, ultimately, to the upward mobility of his descendants.

The Negro found no such warmth. By the time he got to the city, the clubhouse—and City Hall, too—had been castrated. Mayors still got their names in newspapers, but if they tried to do anything about their mounting responsibilities, they discovered, first, that a high proportion of talented citizens had moved out to the minimeadows and, second, that City Hall did not really control the autonomous departments into which urban services had become clotted.

When the government of the city become more efficiently recast in the bureaucratic mold, a terrible price was exacted: there was no longer a whole government to which a whole man could relate. The school system, for example, was a stockade, almost impervious to the wishes of the mayor, the council, the parents, and the electorate. It had a board, supposedly in charge, but since the members of the board were laymen, they were usually front men for the administrators who garrisoned the educational stockade. What instrument of the public will could evaluate how well a school system performed its function? Busily, the educationists evaluated themselves—and rarely found themselves seriously at fault.

So it ran through all the autonomous stockades of public service. When in 1965 John Lindsay was elected Mayor of New York, one of his first big fights was over the degree of control he could exercise over the police department. "Keep City Hall's hands off the police," was the cry of opponents. Remembering the more corrupt past, one can empathize with this attitude. On the other hand, how can the citizen—especially the lowly citizen, the citizen who presents himself for assimilation—how can he mentally and emotionally connect himself to the police if not through City Hall? The lowly citizen had been told this is a democracy; but police departments that ran themselves, school systems that ran themselves, did not seem to fit what he had been told. The antisepsis of bureaucratic municipal government killed a lot of inefficiency and corruption; it killed, too, a lot of connective tissue and nerve ganglia that had previously united citizen and city.

Look at the post-1940 American city from below, from the viewpoint of Mike's successor, Jefferson Truegood, half-literate Negro product of a rural southern school, incompetent as Mike had been incompetent, and, like Mike, bewildered and beset. Who looked at Jeff whole? Who wanted Jeff, even for such selfish reasons as the political bosses and the robber barons of yore had wanted Mike? Who in the governmental power structure of the city was trying to persuade Jeff of anything? Who gave a damn what Jeff thought?

Although the school system was better than it had been in Mike's day, it wouldn't do anything about his children's teeth. That belonged to another department. If the kids started getting into trouble, that was still another department, in blue uniforms—one that didn't really pay any attention to what had happened at school or what hadn't happened in a dentist's chair. There were, too, the social workers, rigidly channeled by law and rule, complex conduits through which welfare money might or might not flow to Jeff, depending on whether in any month his objective circumstances could be squared with a set of standards that neither Jeff nor the social worker had established, and that neither believed in.

Each fragment of the city apparatus assumed that it knew better than Jeff about the corresponding fragment of his life. But Jeff wasn't a fragment, and there was nothing in the structure of the city to which the whole Jeff could attach himself, no point at which he could experience the reciprocal awareness, the mutual trust, of citizen and city.

"Alienation" is an obese word, but it begins to have more pith and point if you get out on the streets and ask Negroes what and whom they hate most. High on their hate list are social workers, teachers, hospital staff—all the people who have been trying to help this fragment or that fragment of a Negro's life. This attitude is, of course, unfair. These people are only doing their jobs, performing services as prescribed by law. But the Negro hates them because they are his points of contact with a system that insists that he travel all the way to meet its terms, a system that has lost its unity, its heart, that will not reach out with warmth toward where he is, a system where municipal institutions are no longer stirred by the great missionary and merchandising cry: "Bring them in!"

Since Mike's day, the city to which Jeff aspired had changed economically even more than governmentally. Mike had had nothing to offer but his muscle—but muscle then was in demand. The economic city gave Mike a meager and precarious living, but its need for Mike was obvious, and its upward paths, though Mike himself would have little chance to tread them, were visibly accessible to his children.

By Jeff's day the muscle market had narrowed and declined. Business, pursuing its own upward mobility, had come to depend more and more on educated workers, inured to industrial discipline. In business, too, specialization and bureaucracy now ruled. Companies become departmentalized, and jobs were defined by rigid sets of special qualifications that applicants had to meet. At the nethermost levels of the employment market, tests frequently screened Jeff out of jobs he could, in fact, perform. By Jeff's day, moreover, it had become harder for Negroes than it had been for members of preceding ethnic groups to found small businesses that might serve as bridges to the larger business world.

The damage done by this exclusion was more than economic. In Mike's day the American business system, in addition to paying Mike, had been one of the great paths of his social and political assimilation to the city. At work Mike learned new forms of joint effort, learned to mingle with men from other lands and with indigenous inhabitants of the city. At work he glimpsed the great lessons of the division of labor, the high social, political, and moral implications of cooperation and competition that underlie the life of trade.

Jeff was shut out from all this—or admitted sporadically and in circumstances that failed to convey to him a sense of opportunity. He could not even tell himself that his children had a solid chance of getting ahead. They were better educated than he, but the economic system kept demanding more and more training; the gap between his children and the system might be as wide as it had been for Jeff himself.

Increasingly, Negroes react with distrust to their rejection by the city. They think they live in the debris of broken promises—the fundamental democratic promise they learned in school and the more recent promises that seemed to be implied by Supreme Court civil-rights decisions and by the War on Poverty. Whites are not the only targets of distrust. One Negro, who has worked in neighborhoods for the Office of Economic Opportunity, put his head in his hands and mourned: "I have completely lost credibility on my turf."

Out of this distrust of white society rose the slogan Black Power. The term has many meanings, some consonant with the idea of the city, some subversive of it. Were the city itself in good health, Black Power might be a natural and wholesome development, a repetition of the experience of many other ethnic groups whose assimilation to America has included the conscious mobilization of their political power. It is natural and wholesome that Negroes, angry at the schools' failure with their children, should seek to control school boards. If Negroes believe that the police harass their race, they have the right to try to take charge, through the ballot box, of the police departments. Perhaps they could teach the whites how to reinvigorate the city's services.

But the city has already deteriorated to the point where no such constructive outcome of rising Negro political power can be expected. In trying to run the cities, Negroes will face the same formidable array of difficulties that the whites have failed to overcome. The day after the election of a Negro mayor in Cleveland, a Negro in another city said: "God help Carl Stokes. Two months after he takes office Cleveland Negroes will be bitter and impatient because Carl hasn't solved their problems."

In its more extreme forms, in the speeches of Stokely Carmichael, for example, Black Power seems to turn its back upon the hope of integration and seeks a separated Negro community. Commenting on this kind of Black Power, Eric Hoffer, philosopher and retired longshoreman, said in a memorable C.B.S. interview, "Nobody can give you power. Power doesn't come in cans. When I hear Carmichael he's always asking, 'Give me the can opener so I'll open the cans of power and eat them.'"

Black Power will mean more segregation, more atomized local sovereignty, more descent toward the anticity, the condition where there is no power because there is no cooperation, no love, no sense of common danger and common destiny. The future of the city will not be served if the housing projects and the slums become stockades of the kind of narrow separatism that permeates the stockades in the minimeadows.

It is deeply significant that the idea of Black Power is already getting in the way of what needs to be done to reconstruct the city. For years, everybody who has looked seriously at the problems of metropolitan areas has known that they needed to be much more closely knit in order to deal with such metropolitan problems as transportation, air pollution, etc. Such common-sense proposals for cooperation have been frustrated for all these decades by the separatism of the upwardly mobile whites in the suburbs who feared that closer political association with the core cities would drag them down. Now—and here's an irony bitter as brass—the Negroes in the core cities are also opposing any form of general metropolitan government, because they fear such proposals would forestall their impending electoral capture of

city halls. "The ghetto," in short, begins to imitate the suburbs. The masters have indeed corrupted the slaves.

Not much has been said here about racial hatred itself as
a danger to the future of the city. Not much will be said, because no man knows how deep and how durable racial hatred
will prove to be. No psychologist has the tools to measure it,
much less the therapy to banish it. We can see, however,
that racial tension has increased because of the deep defects
in the life of the city. We can believe that a contrary process
might be set in motion, that racial tension will diminish and
perhaps disappear if we put our hands, white and black, ear-
nestly to the task of building the practical and spiritual
bridges of community.

We know that when society reaches for him with warmth,
the Negro responds. In Harlem a young white man named
Harv Oostdyk has been running what he calls "street acad-
emies." The idea is to find high-school dropouts and prepare
them for college. It works. Why? What expertise resides in
Oostdyk and his fellows that the school system does not possess? It's not a matter of expertise, but of attitude. Oostdyk
doesn't unlock his door and wait for Negro youths, avid for opportunity, to knock. His people roam the streets and haunt
the pool parlors, looking for prospects. "What our street workers must have is charisma," says Oostdyk. "They have to
get over to the kids the fact that we care."

Oostdyk's approach is marked by a very real respect for
the knowledge already in the heads of Negro dropouts.
"You've got to know a lot to survive on these streets. These
kids know how the numbers game works, what cop is on the
take from whom. Suffering and struggle has built a great foun-
dation in these kids. They have a language, very expressive
and colorful. The school system says forget all that nasty

stuff and don't use your language. Put all that out of your head and let us fill it with something else. The kids won't do it. But if you respect what they know, you can help them to build other knowledge on that. If you respect their language you can teach them ours while you're learning theirs."

Oostdyk thinks he knows a way to bring more of them in. From a battered desk he pulls FORTUNE's list of the five hundred largest U.S. industrial companies. Communicating a vision, he stares at the list and says: "What do these streets know of the world of these companies? What do the people who run these companies know of these streets? The only business you see around here are bars, beauty parlors, fish-and-chips shops. Suppose we could get twenty-five of the biggest corporations into Harlem, each with a storefront or a whole building that says General Motors or Bell Telephone or Standard Oil or General Electric, and inside what's going on are programs—different kinds of programs—for helping these people find themselves. That would put the symbol of American industry back on these streets. It would show the people the way into the structure. Think what that might do for the unity of this country. Think how that might change the way things will be twenty years from now."

The vision of Harv Oostdyk is a remarkably urban vision. It has that vertical reach, that welcome to diversity, that clasp of the unfamiliar, that sweet itch for tomorrow. All of these qualities belonged to the idea of the city before the idea of the city disappeared behind the white picket fences.

Oostdyk's emphasis on the potential role of business in resolving the double crisis is widely echoed. Of course, the more congealed liberals (e.g., John Kenneth Galbraith), whose opinions on this subject entered a zone of permafrost in the 1930's, continue to doubt that business can be the agent of the kind of social advance that is needed. But the leaders of the government of the U.S. believe it. Negroes believe it. Business is the one important segment of society Negroes today do not regard with bitter disillusionment. And thousands of businessmen across the nation, getting involved in the struggle to restore social cohesion, are beginning to lift their sights, to sense that business has indeed a great part to play.

It has, in fact, three parts. The first relates directly to the crisis in relations between the Negro and the rest of U.S. society. Business must reach down for the "unemployable" Negro by lowering its standards of entry, by developing training programs, by making visible and practical the upward career paths Negroes can tread. In the short run, the costs of such efforts will outweigh the return, but modern business willingly incurs many costs that will not come home as revenues for years and years. Looking ahead, an executive can tell his stockholders that he is enriching his supply of future labor—and his future markets. A moral motive is even more pertinent. In the U.S., the role of business is so important that it cannot escape a large share of responsibility for the health of the society.

The second role of business relates to the crisis of the city. Over the last thirty years a tremendously fruitful connection or, as they say, an "interface," has been developed between the corporate world and the federal government. Business has served government well with the products of its innovative spirit—and been handsomely paid. More significant than that, however, is the fact that the general quality of both business and government has been enormously improved by their intimate and massive association.

No such interface exists between the great corporations and the governmental units at the subfederal level. Opening up before us is an era of the "public market" where men will want more and more goods and services of the kind that no individual can buy for himself. His communities will need to buy for him cleaner air and rivers, better scientific research, better techniques of learning, better traffic movement. If these demands are to be met, great corporations will almost certainly play a large part in supplying them.

Across this interface one can see opportunities for the mutual improvement in the quality of corporation life and in the quality of the city. The companies will confirm their reputation of public service, increasingly important to the morale of their employees, especially their technical and managerial staff. The communities will gain a sense of vigor, of forward motion they so grievously now lack.

From this interface there also may evolve greater cohesion between the geographically fragmented communities and between the bureaucratically fragmented services in any community. The federal-corporation interface has developed, in part through systems analysis, powerful techniques to coordinate disparate activities performed by independent centers of decision. One can imagine, say, a private contractor selling an antipollution service to fifty neighboring towns and cities. A dream? Yes, the kind that would be hard reality today if more businessmen and public officials had dreamed it twenty years ago. It would be ironic if we needed systems analysis, computers, and great corporations to help restore the unity of the city, the humanity that the clubhouse boys in their sloppy way attained generations ago.

The third business role in the double crisis gets even closer to the heart of the matter, the nitty-gritty. Big business, the city, and the Negro have something in common: all three are victims of the tyranny of the agrarian myth over the American mind. By publicly taking its stand on the side of the city and the Negro, business can help to restore its own reputation and its own internal morale. The enemies of the business world today cannot gain much rhetorical yardage by denouncing business for sucking the blood of the poor, grinding the faces of the workers, or selfishly holding back the march of progress. Today's indictment of business has its roots in the agrarian prejudice against bigness, complexity, organization, and diversity. Ideals derived from the society of small farmers form the basis for the contemporary smear against business. These accusations hurt. They influence antitrust policy on mergers. They interfere with business efforts to recruit bright young men and women.

Nor is its public repute the most important area in which business suffers at the hands of modern Druids, the tree worshipers. The morale of business is sapped day after day because its managers and its workers live in a society where the dominant myth holds that the ideal human condition is that of the yeoman tilling his own soil, harvesting his own rye, and cooking his own whiskey by the light of his own moon. Such is the power of the myth that many a successful business executive misses some of the relish of business because he feels twinges of guilt at having deserted the simple life.

The big American corporation, looked at as a community, is the American institution nearest in its character to what the city ought to be. The corporation can stretch into any part of the world, deal attentively with any race or culture. It can combine to a unified purpose the most disparate skills, holding internal order amidst the clash of rivalrous opinions. It constitutes a forum and it walks in the marketplace—and these two, forum and market, are the spiritual hallmarks of the city. The corporation can help the Negro join the city, help the city become worthy again of the Negro and the white. Corporation, city, and Negro, forming a natural triple alliance against their common enemy, the modern Druids, can spur the U.S. toward social reconstruction.

In Detroit these days, one can feel the rightness of this alliance. Detroit's business and political leaders are determined to resurrect their city, not just its physically damaged areas, but the immaterial city, the web of human relations, laws, customs, manners, and practices that stretches through that metropolitan area. Suddenly, it seems right and natural that Henry Ford II should walk alone on Twelfth Street to call upon the Reverend Albert Cleage, leader of the Negro militants. It seems right and natural that the heads of the three auto companies should journey to Lansing to lobby vehemently among legislators for an open-occupancy law. It seems right and natural that young Joseph Hudson Jr., of the department-store family, should be spending most of his time on the future of his city, sending missionary speakers to explain core-city problems to suburban meetings and listening carefully to what the Negroes in "the ghetto" want.

Business cannot perform alone the job of rescuing the city. All U.S. institutions, from street gangs to churches, must be involved in the effort. The federal government, especially, will be essential both in providing funds and in keeping public attention fixed on the urgency of the crisis. Much harm was done in the fall of 1967 by congressional threats to cut deeply into antipoverty-program funds; Negroes felt that another promise was being broken. Perhaps the most important new example of federal-local cooperation is the "model cities" program with its stress on the services and functions of the city rather than on bricks and mortar.

No one can foreordain what the material city of the future

35

ought to look like. Perhaps it will be all suburbs. Perhaps it will be a ring around an open space. Its physical shape matters much less than its spiritual character. The actual minimeadows are innocent enough; what imperils our nation are the minimeadows that these symbolize, the minimeadows of the mind. To build the immaterial city we must begin by cleansing ourselves of the inappropriate myth, the value system that clashes with our social nature and our destiny.

Cast down the idols. Level the pious memory of Fort Mims, the bloody stockade on the Tombigbee, built to defend one race against another. Dethrone Daniel Boone, or, at least, so limit, balance, and constitutionalize his mythic monarchy that the American soul will open again to its other dream—not the dream of lonely peak and quiet pond, but the dream of the busy streets, the dream of strangers who become as brothers, the dream of the unfenced society, the dream of the city.

The farm is where we've been; the city's where we're headed. Long, long ago Western man left the woodsy tribal gods for a concept of universal Deity which implies universal brotherhood. This basic change in belief had intellectual and political implications. Gradually, it opened our minds to science and our political institutions to the concepts of diversity and freedom. The American Proposition commits us to the city, to the life of tolerance, to the earnest quest for civic competence, to the forum, to the market, to the society where what we learn can be put to the use of all. We can't turn back. Lingering looks behind only confuse the line of march.

"Like it says in the third chapter of Genesis, if you got this knowledge, man, if you got this power to choose, then you got this serpent, man, this worm of destruction. He'll do you in if you don't choose right."

2

THE
NEW NEGRO
MOOD

by Roger Beardwood

A brand-new set of conditions is emerging in the nation's Negro community. It is less divided in some very important ways than it ever has been in the past. In this new unity, Negroes are drawn together by a sense of progress, and also by a sharply defined, realistic set of objectives—notably, more education for their children, more desegregation, better jobs, and better police protection. Their mood is one of hope mixed with anger, and it is very aggressive; Negroes are more determined than ever to achieve their objectives. As for now, a majority believe in nonviolence, though a sizable minority believe in the tactics of Detroit. Over all, the new mood is basically healthy, for more Negroes are now convinced they must help themselves. And if in the next few years active nonviolence meets with cooperation, and most of all with success, there is a chance that Negro anger and violence will diminish.

These, in the round, are the principal findings of a FORTUNE study of urban Negro attitudes conducted late in 1967 by Daniel Yankelovich, Inc., a New York attitude-research firm. The Negroes interviewed in thirteen cities were encouraged (by Negro interviewers) to talk at length about themselves and their feelings. A number were interviewed in groups and their tape-recorded discussions were used to interpret and explain the tabulations on pages 41 through 43. In addition, FORTUNE conducted a separate group of interviews to provide more insight into the thinking and objectives of the young, the Negro middle class, and the evangelists of violence.

The depth study of Negro thinking has turned up some surprising findings—findings that, when compared with earlier surveys, provide the basis for a somewhat more encouraging outlook than the tumultuous events of the summer of 1967 suggest. Items:

¶ Three out of four Negroes feel their condition is better than it has been in recent years.

¶ Eight out of ten think their chances of getting a good job are better, and on the controversial matter of housing, seven out of ten think conditions have improved.

¶ Three out of four feel more hopeful that Negroes' problems will be solved; a mere 4 percent are less hopeful.

¶ Almost half are more angry than they were a few years ago, and about one in ten is less angry.

¶ A majority endorses the Reverend Martin Luther King's aggressive, nonviolent tactics; but over a third endorse more violent methods. Northern Negroes put somewhat more emphasis on violence than southern urban Negroes do.

The study firmly disposes of a prevalent myth about urban Negroes—that they have little sense of priorities, and small desire to help themselves. Better education for children, better jobs, and more job-related training are almost equally important to poor Negroes and those who are better off, to young and old, and to men and women alike, and to Negroes in the North and South. A second group of objectives also ranks high in importance. A majority want better police protection, better education for themselves, and enough neighborhood improvement to guarantee a better place to live. But only a fifth want to move out of that neighborhood.

The desire to stay in the neighborhood appears to be closely related to new feelings about integration. One Negro in twenty of those interviewed rejects integration as a primary objective; in the sixteen to twenty-five age group, the proportion is nearly double. At the other extreme, about one Negro in ten wants integration in every sense of the word—i.e., believes in the dismantling of all racial barriers. But a substantial majority of urban Negroes—77 percent—opt for what the study calls "limited integration." To them, integration is useful mainly as a means to equal opportunity and increased self-respect.

So up to a point, the study etches a hopeful portrait of a Negro community that has a realistic set of goals, clearly recognizes that progress is being made, and has some confidence that it will continue. But the study also reflects an important ambivalence. Along with recognition that conditions have improved there is that bitterness and anger and a dominant resentment of white people. Some 37 percent say their feelings about whites are better, but 33 percent say they are worse, and 30 percent that their feelings of mistrust have not changed.

Only by looking at Negroes' attitudes toward themselves and their leaders can this mixture of hope and anger be understood. To be sure, most Negroes believe they have more power now than in the past, and many feel they are being treated with greater respect. But the study shows very clearly that most Negroes think they and their leaders have won these improvements from white America by their own efforts. They feel more hopeful about the future precisely because they believe they are winning gains for themselves—and because they are convinced that progress will continue only if they fight for it.

The qualitative part of the study—the open-ended questions, the tape-recorded interviews—throws considerable light on the reasons for this belief in violence. There is, for a start, a strong current of mistrust about the U.S. as it is now run. A majority believes in the ability of the American system to solve Negro problems, but it is a thin majority—and many who express this belief hedge it with reservations. Many of the doubters tend to believe that the promise of America has not been kept so far as Negroes are concerned, and may never be unless they coerce the "white power structure," a phrase that encompasses all the major institutions of the U.S. society.

An important part of the picture—both the bright and the dark one—is that Negroes have found a new pride in themselves. In part this derives, of course, from the real strides that have been made in recent years. The outlawing of desegregation, the opening of new job opportunities, the open-housing laws passed in many communities, and the election of Negroes to political office (more than 700 Negroes hold elective offices), all have raised Negroes in their own and in whites' eyes. But pride also comes from identity with the rise of the independent African nations. And what they see of their leaders and defenders on television has helped many Negroes to achieve a greater degree of belief in themselves.

This pride in black achievement has a backlash. It leads some Negroes—particularly the young—to mistrust a great many things that they have been taught by the white cul-

Text continued on page 44

Opinion poll results on pages 41-43

WHAT
NEGROES THINK

To determine how urban Negroes view their condition, how their view
has changed in the past three to five years and what issues are
important to them, FORTUNE commissioned an in-depth study of the
attitudes held by more than 300 Negroes in thirteen U.S. cities. The
study was conducted by Daniel Yankelovich, Inc., a New York-based firm
specializing in social-science research. The views of the respondents
were obtained by Negro interviewers in October and November, 1967.
Some of the questions were designed to provide answers that could be
counted and tabulated. The main thrust of those findings is shown in the
tables on this and the following pages.* Other questions were designed
to discover why Negroes hold the views they do. Both aspects of the
study are discussed in the chapter that starts on page 37. Footnotes are
on page 43.

FEELINGS ABOUT CONDITIONS NOW VERSUS 3 TO 5 YEARS AGO

Evaluation of over-all conditions:	Better	Worse	About same
Total	73%	10%	17%
16 to 25 years	64	11	25
26 years and over	80	9	11

Comparison of the chances of finding a decent job:	Better	Worse	About same
Total	78%	7%	15%
16 to 25 years	72	7	21
26 years and over	81	8	11

Degree of improvement in housing for Negroes living in the city:	Great	Small	None
Total	37%	32%	29%
Income under $100 a week	44	23	30
Income $100 or more a week	25	44	28

Degree of hope for solving Negro problems:	More	Less	About same
Total	77%	4%	19%
16 to 25 years	74	5	21
26 years and over	78	4	18

Degree of anger about life in the city:	More	Less	Same
Total	46%	12%	42%
16 to 25 years	47	12	41
26 years and over	45	13	42

FEELINGS ABOUT NEEDS

Objectives in the order of their importance:	Total
More education for my children	97%
More desegregation in schools, neighborhoods, jobs	93
A better job	87
Some kind of special training	77
Better police protection	69
More education for myself	62
Making neighborhood a better place to live	60
More money to spend	53
Moving out of the neighborhood	20

Integration as a goal for Negroes:	Total	16-25 years	26 years and over
No—integration of any kind not desirable	5%	9	2
Yes—limited integration wanted, in terms of equal opportunity in jobs, education, and housing	77%	72	81
Yes—total integration wanted on all levels	12%	12	11

FEELINGS ABOUT NEGROES AND WHITES

Changes in degree of power Negroes have:	More	Less	About same
Total	79%	2%	19%
16 to 25 years	75	1	24
26 years and over	82	2	16

How Negroes are treated by whites:	More respect	Less respect	Same
Total	62%	4%	34%
16 to 25 years	60	5	35
26 years and over	62	2	36

How Negroes feel about whites:	Better	Worse	About same
Total	37%	33%	30%
16 to 25 years	34	34	32
26 years and over	39	31	30
Non-South	31	42	27
South[1]	50	15	35

Whether Negroes can get what they want under the U.S. system: [2]	Yes	No	Maybe, Not sure
Total	53%	43%	4%
16 to 25 years	53	45	2
26 years and over	53	42	5
Income under $100 a week	60	39	1
Income $100 or more a week	45	48	7
Non-South	46	51	3
South[1]	67	27	6

FEELINGS ABOUT VIOLENCE AND RIOTING

Whether violence and rioting are necessary to achieve Negro objectives:	Violence necessary	Violence not necessary
Total	**35%**	**62%**
16 to 25 years	40	53
26 years and over	31	68
Men	36	62
Women	32	63
Income under $100 a week	34	61
Income $100 or more a week	36	63
Non-South	44	51
South[1]	14	85

View of the violence and rioting that has already occurred:	Essentially good	Essentially bad	Both good and bad
Total	**14%**	**58%**	**28%**
16 to 25 years	17	54	29
26 years and over	12	60	28
Men	22	46	32
Women	7	68	25
Income under $100 a week	15	58	27
Income $100 or more a week	13	54	33

FEELINGS ABOUT NEGRO LEADERSHIP

How Negro leaders and Negro rights organizations are regarded:

	"Fights for What People Want"				"Is Trusted"			
	Very much	A little	No	Don't know/ No answer	Very much	A little	No	Don't know/ No answer
	%	%	%	%	%	%	%	%
Martin Luther King	83	10	6	1	82	12	4	2
N.A.A.C.P.	70	23	5	2	67	23	5	5
Roy Wilkins	52	32	9	7	52	30	10	8
Thurgood Marshall	49	26	9	16	50	25	8	17
Whitney Young	40	30	10	20	37	30	11	22
CORE	39	36	15	10	37	37	14	12
Stokely Carmichael	32	23	38	7	20	29	43	8
Rap Brown	25	25	40	10	18	28	44	10
Floyd McKissick	24	36	10	30	15	44	10	31
S.N.C.C.	24	38	24	14	20	39	25	16
Adam Clayton Powell	23	37	35	5	25	39	30	6
Black Muslims	15	30	47	8	12	30	47	11

* All figures are percentages. Some "No answers" are not shown and therefore all percentages may not add to 100 percent.

1. Due to the small size of the sample in the South, these figures are shown only as indicators of trends that diverge markedly from those in the North.

2. The replies to this question indicate that many respondents interpreted "the way this country is set up and run" to mean the white man's "establishment." Although their answers were often ambivalent, the thrust of their replies seemed sufficiently striking to warrant inclusion.

ture. One extreme example is rejection of many words in common usage; frequent use of the word black as a synonym for evil or dirt seems evidence enough that the English language has been rigged against them by the white community. They show their pride and their defiance by preferring to be called black instead of Negro.

Many Negroes reason that the current teachings of history in schools and colleges are designed to make them feel inferior and to perpetuate the myth of white superiority. "Black history is the most important thing to me," says John Middleton, a student at Mount Vernon High School, Mount Vernon, New York. "I want to know about myself, you understand? I want to know that there was a Negro cowboy, I want to know that there was famous black people. I want to know black history as far as where I came from—I mean mainly Africa. Nobody learns about blackie. I'm gonna be frank about it. In the 1920's they were giving out degrees to teachers or to people at colleges who could prove that the Negro was inferior, physically and mentally, to other men. This really burns me up."

Many Negroes believe white Americans lie about their attitudes toward black people—and even lie to themselves about those attitudes. Dr. Eugene S. Callender, who resigned in November, 1967 as executive director of the New York Urban League to become deputy administrator of the New York City Housing Development Administration, says: "Whether we know it or admit it or not, white people believe that Negroes as Negroes are inherently inferior. We are all products of a culture which transmits stereotyped racial myths. . . . Who dares to pretend that he transcends centuries and generations of cultural conditioning? Since the time when slavery justified the economic traffic in human beings by rationalizing a myth of racial superiority, we are all tainted by the belief in white supremacy."

There is grisly logic in a black man's believing his condition has improved and in his being angry at the same time. He believes his condition was bad to start with through the fault of white America. Much anger and bitterness center round this feeling of exclusion, of not being quite a citizen yet. "The battle for rights is over and we've won it," says Dr. James Cheek, president of Shaw University in Raleigh, North Carolina. "The battle now is for equality." The majority of Negroes yearn to be accepted as equals in the mainstream of society, and the real turmoil in the black community is over the best strategy to achieve that objective. It is a turmoil that afflicts every class and virtually every institution. Fundamentally, the issue is one of faith. Can America as it is now run solve the problems of black people? Does it really desire to solve them? The study suggests that a majority still answer those questions with a yes—but often a tremulous yes. And those who have lost faith, the militant black nationalists, are expressing a mood shared by many people, particularly the young.

The medium that has made Negroes more aware of the gap between their condition and that of whites, television, is also the medium that carries the message of the militants loudest and clearest. The fulminations of a Rap Brown or Stokely Carmichael make TV news. The measured, rebutting cadences of a Whitney Young or Roy Wilkins are less likely to be shown at peak viewing hours. Nobody, not even militant spokesmen themselves, can say with any certainty how many members there are in uncounted militant Negro organizations; the more relevant question is how many accept both the strategy of militance and the tactic of violence.

The militants do not agree among themselves on the ultimate objectives of their programs. Many of them want to use violence to speed their progress into full membership in American society. But others, a small but growing minority, are advocates of separatism—the idea that black Americans should have their own state within the U.S. Like some of the militants, the evangelists of separatism frequently quote the late Frantz Fanon, a West Indian psychiatrist and leading intellectual of the Algerian revolution, to demonstrate that black Americans differ from other oppressed non-white peoples only by being a colony inside the U.S. To justify their suspicion of white attempts to help Negroes, and of Negroes who accept those overtures, they often refer to this key passage from Fanon's *The Wretched of the Earth:* "As it develops, the war of liberation can be counted upon to strike a decisive blow at the faith of the leaders. The enemy, in fact, changes his tactics. At opportune moments, he combines his policy of brutal repression with spectacular gestures of friendship, maneuvers calculated to sow division. . . . Here and there he tries with success to revive tribal feuds, using *agents provocateurs* and practicing what might be called countersubversion." Fanon's message to many militants: white efforts to improve the condition of black men are merely attempts to split black unity; and the appointment of black men to positions of apparent influence in the white power structure is an attempt to buy off opposition to white policies.

The message of the separatists, of course, is not new. Separatism is a recurring theme in American Negro history that strikes responsive chords in the minds of those who feel they are doomed to continued victimization by whites. Furthermore, some believers in separatism—whether in a separate state, or in separate urban Negro communities—fear that if they attempt to compete in a white man's world on his terms they will inevitably fail. There are grounds for that fear. Though catching up, Negroes are still badly behind whites in education, and they approach many jobs well knowing that the intellectual cards are stacked against them. Many who do not believe in permanent separatism of any kind do believe, however, that the Negroes should think and develop as black people, and not accept white models of behavior and aspiration.

This issue—whether to live in the white world or the black—has peculiar poignance for the middle class, whose goals in the past have often seemed to be lifted straight from the pages of *House Beautiful*. But now there is increasing evidence that middle-class Negroes are identifying more with the black community. "When they start talking about Negroes, I say I'm a Negro too," says Leon Coward, director of a Day Care Center in New York City. "But my brother down there, he could kick me in the pants, 'cause he knows I've got a bellyful, and his is empty. Now we're getting to the point where I am beginning to recognize this man's empty belly."

William Manney, sales manager for W.B.E.E., a Negro-oriented radio station in Chicago, says: "The new thinking is to go into the area of economic power. Let's say they're gonna boycott a store. They figure out what's the man's margin of profit, what they represent to him in dollars and cents. There they control his vitals. In controlling his vitals, they also control his behavior. The so-called bourgeois Negroes are trying to educate their brothers how to fight this man in the same way that he's been doing us for years. We'll educate our people to realize just how much we mean to him. Black power means to have a piece of the pie."

In the slang of the slums, this is "green power," and in scores of cities Negroes are now working toward "economic self-development." Green power means, simply, that Negroes want to own more businesses in primarily black neighborhoods, own more of the real estate, and feed more black spending power into black pockets. Much of the emotional support of the drive toward "green power" is provided by the poor themselves; but when it comes to translating that emotional content into action, the middle class is in the forefront. And the middle class is likely to be so for some time, says Livingston Wingate, the controversial former director of a Harlem anti-poverty program, New York City's federally supported HARYOU-ACT. "The potency of poverty is such that it takes from a man the hope, vigor, and self-respect he needs to remedy his own ailment," says Wingate. "If he is to remedy it, he needs all the help he can get: white and black, and from the middle class. This assistance, however, must come in terms that are compatible with the dignity and self-respect of the poor."

Harlem already has a model project designed to give the people themselves the power to decide through democratic methods what they want, then to implement those decisions with the help of specialists. Created by HARYOU-ACT, Neighborhood Boards have been set up, with members elected by the people of Harlem. An important function of the boards is to evolve a development plan for Harlem; the hope is that the boards will eventually provide local government for the area, something some experts regard as vital if the social problems of Harlem are to be solved.

The gulf between the views of Negroes living in the cities of the North and West and those in the urban South is now wider than ever in some important respects. Southern urban

Negroes are, according to FORTUNE's questionnaire,
—more hopeful that Negro problems can be solved
—less mistrustful of white people
—less disposed toward the use of violence in the pursuit of their objectives.

The distinctive Negro mood in the South was suggested in the summer of 1967, when the relative peace in southern cities contrasted sharply with the turmoil in the urban North. The different mood in the urban South also showed up clearly in the interviews conducted for FORTUNE's 1967 study of urban Negro attitudes—even though the study was not designed for the making of statistical comparisons or, in most instances, reporting results by regions.

The new Negro mood is based on a greater sense of improvement in living conditions, a greater degree of faith in the system to produce future progress, and a greater sense that what has been achieved so far is the result of Negroes' nonviolent efforts. In sum, southern urban Negroes, even though still worse off in absolute terms, tend to be more satisfied with the rate of change and less aggressive than Negroes in the North.

There are several reasons for the relative contentment of Negroes in the urban South. One is that expectations were lower in the South than they were in the North and West, and those expectations are being met—so far. Another vital factor is the relationship between the races. Shocking though it may sometimes seem to white Northerners, the characteristic bluntness of white Southerners in racial matters is sometimes approved by Negroes—and remembered with some nostalgia by southern-born Negroes living in the North.

In the South, half the Negroes interviewed felt better now about white people than they did three to five years ago. In the non-South, only one out of three felt better. Better feelings about whites are closely related to feelings about Negroes' sense of their own power: more Negroes in the South than in the non-South think they have greater power than they did in the past. One reason for that different appreciation of power derives, of course, from the contrasts between life in southern and northern cities.

All too often, the southern migrant's hopes are frustrated by harsh economic and social realities in the Negro slums of the North and West. Familiar communal patterns of Negro life and the personal contact Negroes have with whites in the South seem lacking to a southern Negro in the large cities of the North. Some southern-born migrants interviewed complained of feeling adrift and powerless.

In the South, on the other hand, Negroes have remained within the social structure, while making real gains for themselves with relatively less help from whites. The study suggests that strong feelings of self-achievement are a powerful factor in the new assurance and confidence of southern urban Negroes. It also suggests that if the rate of progress continues a tenable solution to the Negro-white problem may yet be found in the South.

Traditionally, an alternative to trying to change the ways of this world was offered by the emphasis of Negro fundamentalist churches on the promise of the next one. The churches are still a potent force in the black community. But the new, aggressive mood of Negroes, and their newfound pride in themselves, have forced many changes on the churches. Their view of man is changing, and with it the Negro's view of God and of himself. "The Negro church in the past was preparing us to die," says Ron Sampson, a Chicago advertising executive. "Not to live—to die. But I am not so much concerned about my burdens being lifted after I'm gone. I want to lift them now. I want my religion to prepare me to live in the hell that's here."

In response to the new religious needs, many Negro ministers are altering their own conception of their role; that old-time religion is clearly out of fashion, particularly with the young. In many cities, black ministers are in the front line of the battle for civil and economic rights; last fall some 700 Negro ministers meeting in Dallas formed themselves into a committee intended to help black people win more control in the here and now. "In the last seven years my views have changed radically," says the Reverend Arthur M. Brazier, minister of the Apostolic Church of God (Pentecostal) on the South Side of Chicago, and president of the Woodlawn Organization. "We must be concerned with the whole man now, not just with his soul. The churches are going to be forced to adapt themselves to what is happening. They are going to take a more positive position on social issues. If they don't, they will lose their influence."

In white ears, the call for black power may sound menacing, whether it comes from the pulpit or the pool hall. But for Negroes answering questionnaires late in 1967, black power expresses real and pressing needs. They are for Negroes to have more control over their own lives, to be able to choose between occupations freely, and to make the places where they live more pleasant. In their own minds, Negroes feel they have gone a long way toward achieving that right to decide: 79 percent feel they have more power now than three to five years ago, 19 percent feel they have the same amount, and 2 percent feel they have less. But an appetite for power is hard to slake: the majority of black people still do not feel they have enough power by a long shot. And the use of "white" funds to aid poor people can in itself emphasize black people's comparative lack of power; many Negroes express strong resentment that the money is frequently spent as white people think it should be, not as black people feel they need it.

The generations of powerlessness and frustration account for much of the anger and apparent exaggeration that so many Negroes express. To white people, indeed, Negroes' use of the word ghetto to describe the neighborhoods in which they live often seems an exaggeration: many of those neighborhoods are not ghettos in any classic sense of the word. But as a Detroit lawyer said, sitting in his new two-story home far from the poor-black area, "The ghetto is inside our heads, because America is our ghetto of the spirit. We're third-class citizens here, and don't you forget it. And it's no good telling us, 'Be patient. The Irish made it eventually.' Baby, we've been here longer than the Irish, and we still haven't made it. Know why? Because you can lose your Irish accent and change your name from O'Riordan to Lodge, but I can't get this blackface make-up off."

Power is the name of the game, and lack of that power the root cause of Negro discontent. Negroes rate very highly housing, jobs, education, money, medical care, and the material ingredients of life. But the real importance of those objectives is that they symbolize entry into the mainstream of American life. And they want full entry passionately. Most Negroes take very seriously the American dream of freedom, justice, and opportunity for all. The battle within the Negro community is between those who believe they can still share in that dream without using violence, and those who do not. Those who reject violence have in abundance one peculiarly American quality, belief that in America a just cause will eventually triumph.

3

BUSINESS RECLAIMS HUMAN RESOURCES

by Gilbert Burck

In the mid-1960's Laurens, South Carolina, looked like the kind of place industry was searching for. Many of its residents were unemployed or underemployed, and the pine forests around town were full of folk, mostly Negro but many white, who had so effectively isolated themselves from the world that they had never been included in a census. Among the companies that located in or near Laurens were several clothing factories, the American Lava subsidiary of Minnesota Mining & Manufacturing, and Monsanto. But the new industries hadn't been there very long before they began to complain of a shortage of qualified labor. The unemployed of Laurens and its environs were so close to being illiterate they couldn't pass the basic employment tests.

Laurens County officials applied to the Office of Economic Opportunity for money for a demonstration project, and got an initial grant of $96,500. To manage the project they called on U.S. Research & Development Corp. of New York, an organization that both administers joint government-industry programs for alleviating unemployment and gives courses in "human resource development"—i.e., it teaches the unemployed how to behave in applying for and holding a job. To run a ten-week course in basic reading and arithmetic for Laurens "unemployables," U.S.R. & D. hired MIND, Inc. (meaning Methods of Intellectual Development), a private company that has used its own new teaching methods to achieve remarkable results in improving basic scholastic abilities. A run-down mansion was rented and converted into an Industrial Education Center, and there U.S.R. & D. and MIND set up shop.

In April, 1967, the center placed spot announcements of the course on local radio stations and a few ads in the local paper. More than 450 people responded. Some were completely illiterate, while others were well enough educated to hope they might earn a high-school diploma. Eighty were chosen; to the dismay of MIND, their average I.Q. was lower than the 75 that it had specified as a minimum. Nevertheless, seventy-two completed the ten-week course in July, 1967; and sixty-eight, including twenty-one who had been on relief, got jobs. J. P. Southerland, executive vice president of the First National Bank, estimates that the program created about $140,000 in yearly take-home pay. "It was like a small industry locating here," he says.

Laurens is only one of many similar recent achievements. U.S. business, in its first tentative steps to struggle with the problem of Negro unemployment, has already shown that it can be amazingly successful in the field of education. It has made enough progress, moreover, to suggest that it may not only junk some of its own shopworn standards of qualification and training, but may challenge the traditional, time-encrusted first principles of the educational establishment.

The bulk of the physically able unemployed, white as well as black, now consists of the "hard core" unemployed and the wholly or "functionally" illiterate—in short, society's rejects and dropouts, the kind who literally came out of the woods at Laurens. About half are sixteen to twenty-four, and are largely concentrated in the metropolitan areas. Most are products of an educational system that has left some 20 percent of the population functionally illiterate. It has also forced Negroes in particular to compete with children better able to relate their studies to their environment. These lost souls, identifying formal education with failure, are often paralyzed by the very thought of teachers and classrooms. They feel secure only in the prison of the slums, which they perforce hate all the more. Many who have managed to get high-school diplomas possess only seventh-grade reading and ciphering abilities. Some dropouts have only the vaguest notion of what punctuality or time means, and cannot even make themselves understood to outside worldlings. All too many suffer from an almost total lack of motivation, or the ability to relate their efforts to anything the outside world counts as worth while.

As some Laurens County businessmen have found out, however, most of these outcasts possess more than enough innate ability to hold down useful jobs and to advance to better ones. A major reason they have not been able to demonstrate such abilities is that they have been screened out of job after job by competitive tests that rarely if ever were designed to uncover the potential of people like themselves. It now looks as if business, and business alone, simply by finding a way of including them in its standard practice of identifying ability with performance, can reclaim most of the human resources that have been all but lost in city and rural slums.

The physical dimensions of the job ahead are not colossal. About 650,000 or 7.4 percent of the non-white labor force is unemployed; to bring the figure down to the white level of

3.3 percent, as former Secretary of Commerce Alexander Trow-bridge pointed out, business would have to create fewer than 350,000 jobs for Negroes. On paper, this is not a Herculean task for an economy that is already creating 1,500,000 jobs a year. It is true that jobs alone are not the cure for Negro un-rest. But without economic jobs—as distinguished from make-work jobs—all else is of little avail. The payoff could be immense. Putting only 350,000 "unemployable" Negroes to work, provided, of course, other employment is not reduced, would add more than $1 billion annually to the national out-put and subtract millions from its welfare costs.

The departments of Labor and Justice and the Equal Em-ployment Opportunity Commission keep complaining that too many companies are still hiring too few Negroes and advanc-ing even fewer. They are indeed. The good news is that more and more companies are now working hard both to hire and to promote "non-whites." The newly formed Urban Coalition, which consists of more than 1,200 business, labor, religious, civil-rights, government, and other leaders, has strongly com-mitted itself "to programs instead of promises." Dozens of corporate programs are under way or in the planning stage. And many companies with ambitious programs, not wanting to seem to promise anything they cannot deliver, are wisely re-fusing to discuss them yet. Fair warning: the movement has its troubles and will doubtless run into more. But it is certainly showing how business can train and employ the "unemploy-ables" once it puts its mind to the job.

A good example is the Watts Manufacturing Co., estab-lished in August, 1966, in the riot-torn Watts district of Los Angeles by Aerojet-General, a subsidiary of General Tire & Rubber Co. Dan A. Kimball, the chairman of the executive committee of Aerojet-General, had lived in Watts as a boy; and when Vice President Humphrey, after the riots of 1965, called on business to make work for Watts residents, Kimball responded at once by selling his colleagues on a scheme for hiring some of them. Mainly because of union and seniority problems, Aerojet-General decided to set up an independent operation in Watts. At first the company intended to make electrical components, but then decided to go in for something that took less skill. Its policy, however, was not to take "in-house" orders, but to bid for contracts in the open market. Its first contract was with the government, for $2,500,000 worth of fifty-two-foot tents that the military needed in a hurry. So Kimball hired some women with heavy sewing experience and went into the tent business.

The personnel director, himself a Negro, did not test for knowledge or skills, but hired practically all who applied. More than 80 percent of the 440 people he hired had no real work experience, and more than half had police records. Yet pilferage was not abnormally high. At first absenteeism was appalling, up to 35 percent on Monday mornings. But the work was simple, and sympathetic instruction helped employees gradually to do a job in which they could take a certain pride. The company also introduced a piecework incentive system that enabled ambitious people to earn as much as $25 a day. Thus it reduced absenteeism to 8 percent. Turnover is still high—6 percent a month against a normal 2 percent—but happily it is high mainly because many employees have improved themselves enough to get better-paying jobs elsewhere. Since there is plenty of manpower in Watts, this was not a major handicap. Many of the more ambitious who stayed on were promoted; one man who hadn't worked in five years became a supervisor.

The Watts workers, in short, had no skills and little knowledge, but when motivated they learned fast. Productivity has improved remarkably, from one tent a day per employee to twenty-two, enabling the company to bid successfully against low-cost producers in the rural South. It has got contracts for tents, metal parts, and wooden shipping crates. It has a backlog of no less than $2,500,000, and hopes to employ as many as 900. And the company has reached the breakeven point—much earlier than planned.

Kimball believes that other companies should "multiply" the Watts model; and partly on the strength of its success, William E. Zisch, vice chairman of Aerojet-General, was appointed special assistant to Secretary of Commerce Trowbridge. Zisch's job is to persuade business, particularly in metropolitan areas with hard-core unemployed, to hire more Negroes. The federal government, through various agencies, is underwriting the "extra" cost of such projects by paying for training, guaranteeing leases, subsidizing mass transportation, and contacting the hard-core unemployed. Zisch, an almost ferociously resourceful man, surely cannot be accused of resting on his oars. He has talked or written to the executives of every one of FORTUNE's list of the 500 leading U.S. corporations, and has divided them into three groups: the Heroes, the Blue Ribbons, and the Unmentionables. The first of the Heroes was Avco, which is establishing a project, with a federal training grant of $1,148,000 and a direct investment of $2,300,000, to employ 200 to 250 hard-core unemployed in the Roxbury section of Boston. Control Data has made a commitment for a similar project, while Goodyear, General Dynamics, and Northrop are contemplating the idea.

Watts Manufacturing obviously is a kind of tour de force that hardly can be copied on a scale big enough to employ at least 350,000 Negroes. It partly avoids the education problem by making products that demand little employee education, and avoids the problems of mixing Negroes with existing white labor by running what amounts to a segregated operation. Significantly, Zisch's national program emphasizes hiring the hard-core unemployed and training them for the job.

One of the pioneers in educating dropouts and functional illiterates is a nonprofit organization known as the Board for Fundamental Education, headquartered in Indianapolis. B.F.E. was founded in 1948 by Dr. Cleo W. Blackburn, then executive director of a settlement house in Indianapolis. Blackburn is executive director; Charles A. Meyer, vice president of Sears, Roebuck, is president and H. Bruce Palmer of the National Industrial Conference Board is chairman. B.F.E. has for more than a decade devoted itself to helping undereducated people of all races—not only with on-the-job education but with "self-help" housing and community health programs. For a long time it worked mostly with state and local governments and other organizations including the National Association of Manufacturers. Late in 1965 it began to sell its services to corporations; its first industrial client was Diamond Alkali, where it supplements the company's many special training programs with basic education courses.

B.F.E.'s expansion into industry aims not only to upgrade workers on the job but to root their improvement in self-esteem and pride. "They've failed in school," Dr. Blackburn tells his prospects. "The best place to learn is in the world of work." B.F.E.'s chief tool, developed and tried out experimentally by its adult education and research director, Dr. R. Lee Henney, is an on-the-job educational method he calls Systems for Success. The method teaches reading, writing, spelling, arithmetic, and basic English grammar with texts that relate these subjects to the job. There are four two-hour sessions a week, and Henney tries to get away from the inhibitions of competitive classrooms by using teachers as moderators rather than as drillmasters. The system is calculated to bring an employee to the fourth-grade level in 150 classroom hours or about twenty weeks, to the eighth-grade level in another 150 hours, and to high-school "equivalency" in perhaps another 400 hours. Blackburn claims that the cost of B.F.E.'s on-the-job education (about $300 for 150 hours per person) is actually less than the cost of going out in today's tight labor market and screening dozens to get the "right" person.

B.F.E.'s classes, which in early 1968 had more than 25,000 enrolled, have trained more than 80,000 workers, as well as 4,000 teachers; Blackburn says that B.F.E. is ready to train as many as a million workers. Among its clients are Du Pont, Olin Chemical, and Eastman Kodak; in May, 1967, it signed a "historic" pilot-project contract with seven major steel companies for raising the achievement levels of 1,600 steel workers in Baltimore and Gary. The cost will be assumed by the departments of Labor and of Health, Education and Welfare, under provisions of the Manpower Development and Training Act (MDTA) of 1962.

B.F.E.'s industrial progress, recent as it has been, has appropriately enough generated a competitor—and a competitor that proposes nothing less than to make a profit both for itself and the companies it works for. The new company goes by the name of MIND, Inc.; its activities in Laurens have already been chronicled. MIND is the creation of a bright man named Charles F. Adams, who had worked in Army intelligence and as a private investment consultant before the National Association of Manufacturers hired him and several others to identify industry's major problems in the years to come. Adams correctly decided that one of business' most important problems would be to provide basic training that the public school system was obviously not providing. This brought him into contact with B.F.E. and Dr. Henney. After studying Henney's system, Adams characteristically decided it could be improved.

The B.F.E. system shuns many conventional classroom methods, but is nevertheless based on the assumption that contact with a trained teacher is good for people who were poor students as children. Adams devised a system that almost does away with the usual classroom and all its connotations of failure. He simply tapes the lessons and the student plugs his earphones into a tape machine. To put the student in a relaxed mood, lessons are accompanied by soft music. Basic arithmetic lessons, for the pupil who can count to ten but cannot add, allow him ten seconds to count on his fingers before writing the answers on his pad.

Successive lessons narrow the time interval, but if the student repeats the lesson nobody laughs at him or raps him on the knuckles. If he speeds up, nobody accuses him of being a teacher's pet. There are no teachers. There are only monitors, who check errors and help students who want help.

By the summer of 1966, Adams had successfully tried out parts of his system on New York City slum "unemployables," and then set out to sell it to the business world. His sales pitch was simply that he would bring the rejected and disadvantaged up to employable levels at less than their selection cost—i.e., the cost of advertising for, interviewing, and testing the average nonprofessional worker. His former boss at N.A.M., Bennett E. Kline, had left to join Corn Products Co., so Adams took his system to Corn Products.

The company's Argo complex at Summit, Illinois, fifteen miles southwest of Chicago, is probably the world's biggest food-processing plant; it employs 3,500, about half "non-white." Argo's problem was not a shortage of applicants, but a shortage of workers who could qualify for available jobs, practically all of which required, as the minimum, an ability to read and cipher at the fifth-grade level. Argo had to reject nine out of ten applicants, and the cost of weeding out this discouraging army of educational bankrupts was beginning to hurt. Furthermore, many of Argo's regular employees did not have enough education to advance to more complex jobs, to say nothing of supervisory and management jobs.

At a price of $250 per head, MIND got astounding results with a group of thirty-eight workers, average age forty-two, who had fourth- and fifth-grade arithmetic abilities and vocabularies. During seventy-nine hours of two-hour sessions four times a week, these Argo employees increased their word knowledge by an average of 2.6 grades, their spelling by 2.2 grades, and their arithmetic by 3.2 grades. To put it another way, for every 7.9 hours under MIND instruction, they increased their academic skills by the equivalent of 2.2 to 3.2 months in school. Functionally illiterate workers have already been moved up several levels, with appropriate pay increases.

Corn Products directors were so impressed that they voted to take over MIND and operate it as a subsidiary of the company, with Adams as its president. Since then MIND has expanded its work at Argo to take in more than 100 people in the plant, and expects to use it soon on job applicants. It also tried out its arithmetic system on ten backward local high-school students, and in only twenty hours of work improved their performance by nearly a grade and a half.

Adams and Kline, who now work together, aren't confining MIND's teaching to reading and arithmetic. They have developed a course in typing that has proved to be enormously successful, and have sold it to more than twenty large companies, and have other things in mind. Kline, indeed, talks about "beating" the public school system. "As things stand, it would take the system fifty years to revolutionize itself," he says. "We can do it in two." MIND has signed up fifty companies, including I.B.M., Procter & Gamble, Crown Zellerbach, and Chrysler, and aims for a $10-million business by its fifth year. Many outsiders are understandably skeptical; such success seems too sudden to be durable. Adams and Kline, for their part, are aware they are bound to encounter problems and even setbacks. "But our biggest problem to date," Kline laments, "is to persuade prospects to believe us."

Corporations with large defense contracts have perforce been actively hiring Negroes and other minorities, and none perhaps has been more active than Lockheed Aircraft. Lockheed was the first to join Plans for Progress, an association formed early in the Sixties to promote equal employment opportunity; and Eugene G. Mattison, Lockheed's personnel director, served for a time as the organization's administrative director. Lockheed itself has an experimental program for hiring and training the hard-core unemployed in its aerospace plants in Sunnyvale, California, and Marietta, Georgia. "Motivation is the key," says Mattison. "These people simply don't believe what you tell them; they think what you're offering is just another chance to fail. You have to persuade them that notwithstanding any disappointments they've had, there's really something for them now if they prepare themselves, apply themselves, and work. That isn't easy."

At least 75 percent of Lockheed's candidates are non-whites and at least 25 percent have police records. At Marietta the program is partly financed by a $300,000 MDTA contract, but at Sunnyvale, owing to local union objections to the program, the project is paid for largely by the company. Candidates for training at Sunnyvale are referred to Lockheed by local agencies such as the Opportunities Industrialization Center-West, the Urban League, East Bay Skills Center, and others that screen the men and give them three to four weeks of basic pre-vocational training, including reading, writing, and arithmetic, grooming, hygiene, and some "motivational" talks. On Lockheed's payroll they go through four more weeks of basic training—how to handle tools, how to conduct themselves, how to use the time clock. After that they spend six weeks at fabricating and assembly jobs, where they use simple machines or hand tools. Finally they are assigned to a regular job classification, but six months later they must go back to class for a week of refresher training. Of the forty-five men who started training at Sunnyvale in January, 1967, only one had to be sacked; the Sunnyvale plant trained a total of 100 hard-core unemployed in 1967 and planned to train 200 in 1968.

At Marietta, candidates are recruited from the community with the help of the Urban League, the N.A.A.C.P., and others. However, they are provided no pre-vocational training to weed out untrainables. By September, 1967, ninety men, of whom sixty-eight were from minority groups and thirty-four had police records, had been enrolled in the program. Twenty-five flunked out; of the sixty-five who survived the training, three have been promoted, one of them twice. Marietta also planned to train 200 people in 1968.

Hiring and training dropouts for relatively low-paying office jobs seems to be more difficult than hiring and training them for factory work, as the Equitable Life Assurance Society can testify. Equitable's home office in New York employs some 7,500 people, more than 70 percent of whom are young and nubile female clerical workers. Turnover has always been high; Equitable regularly hired 1,000 to 1,200 young people each June as they graduated from high school. It interviewed and tested thousands and picked the best of the lot. By the early 1960's, owing in part to the vast increase in New York City's Negro and Puerto Rican population, school standards were declining steeply; and the company was forced to take young people with less and less real education and spend a lot of money training them to its standards. And even as qualified prospects became scarce, more employees than usual left to get better jobs elsewhere. Equitable's turnover soared.

In 1962, Chairman James F. Oates Jr., who was then serving on the President's Committee on Youth Employment, decided to experiment with hiring dropouts, both because he felt obliged to and because he hoped the dropouts would be less inclined to quit once they had a good job. With the help of the New York State Employment Service and JOIN ("Job Orientation in Neighborhoods," a government agency) Equitable scaled down its conditions for employment, excluding categorically only youths with I.Q.'s of less than ninety, narcotics addicts, and perverts. It paid little attention even to police records. No bonding company, at first, would insure these dropouts, and Equitable had to take the responsibility; now the bonding companies cover them after they have worked with Equitable for two years.

The first experiment, in 1962 and 1963, was not very encouraging. The company took on twenty boys, of whom thirteen were dismissed or had left within a year, some for better jobs. Learning from its errors and omissions, Equitable did considerably better with the 1964 group of twenty-four boys and the 1965 and 1966 groups of forty-two boys and thirty-five girls. Unmarried mothers, incidentally, proved to be the best motivated of all of the dropout employees. By the end of 1967, the company had hired 121 dropouts, eighty-five boys and thirty-six girls. It had dismissed thirteen girls and twenty-seven boys; fifteen girls and thirty boys resigned; and thirteen boys were drafted. So of the 121, only twenty-three were still employed.

Equitable is not discouraged. The major reason for dismissals was tardiness and absenteeism, which ran to about 30 percent for the dropouts, against a normal 3 to 4 percent. "You can't explain to your other employees why dropouts can get away with things the rest aren't allowed to do," remarks Edward Chave, second vice president in charge of manpower. The malingering, of course, is the result of little experience in living by the clock, bad housing, and the dogmatic boredom that seems to afflict all the unmotivated. Equitable accordingly is making shift to deal with these fundamentals. Realizing that the dropouts must be allowed to experience success, it is educating its supervisors accordingly. It is running programs on a two-year basis, and adopting a policy of taking on unmarried mothers. Personnel counselors who enjoy the dropouts' confidence take a certain responsibility for keeping them on the job. Equitable also has retained the Board for Fundamental Education to supplement its own training program with courses designed to bring its sub-educated up to high-school "equivalency" levels.

Metropolitan Life Insurance Co., whose New York home office employs 18,000 people, mostly girls, has been somewhat more successful with dropouts because it has been more selective in hiring them. Traditionally, Metropolitan hired no one without a high-school diploma, and traditionally its "Little Marys" or candidates for marriage have resulted in a large turnover. By the end of 1967, however, the company had hired no fewer than 700 dropouts who applied for jobs.

Metropolitan has also taken on dropouts selected by the Urban League, Mobilization for Youth, and JOIN, in batches of a dozen or so. But Metropolitan hires them only if they pass a "native potential" test. They are brought in as trainees and are paid $1.50 an hour; as such they spend four hours a day on the job learning clerical work and two hours in informal "self-development" classes designed to improve their reading and arithmetic skills. Metropolitan has raised trainees' achievement levels by two grades in thirteen weeks, and their self-confidence level immeasurably, with the result that 60 percent have made good. "While all such trainees need to improve their academic skills," says Vice President Karl Kreder, "we found something of even greater importance: they all need to gain the confidence that comes with achieving something."

Metropolitan chose about twenty-five young Negro and Puerto Rican employees who are making good and sent them around to high schools as "living witnesses" of the fact that "minority" employees can get ahead in the company. The living witnesses do not actively recruit for Metropolitan, but demonstrate to the students that the easiest way to land a good job is to earn a diploma in the first place.

Partly because Detroit is 35 percent Negro, the auto industry for years has employed its share of Negroes. As long ago as 1946, some 12,000, or 17 percent, of Chrysler's hourly employees were "non-white" (i.e., practically all Negro), and although few Negroes were then on the corporate salary payrolls, the company began to upgrade them. In its bad years Chrysler had to lay off a lot of people and to observe seniority priorities in rehiring them—i.e., whites usually got back first. But it began to help Negroes in other ways, such as training those on its rolls for promotion. In 1963, Chrysler signed up its first Negro dealer, Ed Davis of Detroit. In 1964, no longer confronted with large lay-off rolls, it intensified its hiring and promotion policies; within three years it promoted 263 hourly rated non-whites to foremen, 115 to skilled trades, 78 to supervisory management and executive jobs, and 98 to corporate salary rolls. As of 1967, 32,700, or more than 23 percent, of its employees were non-white.

In the same period, General Motors reported that 12.4 percent, or 63,000, of its U.S. employees were non-white (Ford does not divulge such statistics). Both Ford and G.M. are upgrading Negroes and recruiting from Negro colleges and schools. Henry Ford II was the first industry man to contribute to Detroit's Career Development Center, founded by Alvin W. Bush, a Negro ex-bellhop, and a schoolteacher named Mrs. Irma Craft, to train Negroes for jobs, help them find jobs, and in general to develop positive attitudes. The industry has contributed more than $170,000 to the center, and is aiding with equipment and professional staff.

In October, 1967, Ford decided that the only way to get the outcasts was to go right into the slums for them and waive the usual examinations. "We screened them in, not out," one official puts it. Ford moved in two slum hiring stations and asked applicants only to fill out a form and pass a physical examination. If they could do both and were not dope addicts or habitual criminals, Ford hired them on the spot. In all, it hopes to take on between 4,000 and 6,000. To tide them over till payday, it gives them books of bus tickets and advances them lunch money.

General Motors, which for some time had used a "rule of

reason" in hiring marginal workers, presently went even further. Working with the Urban League, it established what it called Project Opportunity, which committed it not only to hire several hundred so-called unemployables, but to refrain, for a time, from firing them for tardiness, absence, or lack of ability. If a worker fails to show up, one of a follow-up committee goes to the malingerer's house, hauls him out of bed, and delivers him to the factory; if the worker has personal problems, he is directed to agencies that help solve them. Of the 250 people General Motors hired in Pontiac under this arrangement, 182 or 73 percent were still on the job at the beginning of 1968. Very much encouraged, G.M. is repeating the experiment in Chevrolet's Detroit gear-and-axle plant.

So far, these people have received little or no training; if a man can read a few words, he can be shown how to do a repetitive assembly-line job. Many automobile men, however, feel that they and the industry will benefit if these new workers are given some supplementary education. Chrysler has contracted for courses with MIND, and has also given a substantial grant to the Detroit Industrial Mission, which is analyzing the industry's turnover and motivation problems.

One of the Negro auto worker's major vexations is that he often has to spend hours traveling from home to work and back again, and the auto companies are at last getting behind state open-housing legislation that presumably will enable Negroes to live closer to work. Ford and Chrysler have posted representatives at Lansing, the state capital; some legislators allude to Stewart Didzun, the Ford lobbyist, as "Rap" Didzun and to Hiram Todd, the Chrysler lobbyist, as "Stokely" Todd. And in October, 1967, G.M. Chairman James Roche himself flew up to Lansing to plead the cause of open housing before an unenthusiastic legislature. A youthful black agitator also went along and spoke his mind freely, alluding to legislators and auto executives alike as fat cats.

As business assumes more and more responsibility for hiring and training dropouts, it seems bound to run into difficulties with what the bureaucrats like to call the interface between industry and government. A good example is Newark's Project SEED (meaning Skills Escalation and Employment Development) and its satellite programs, established in 1966 to train unemployed or underemployed residents of disadvantaged neighborhoods for a variety of jobs in metalworking, a trade that accounts for a large percentage of industrial employment in and around Newark.

SEED is a joint government-industry operation. The departments of Labor, Commerce, and Health, Education and Welfare, working with the New Jersey State Employment Service, granted $1,108,335 to the project, and so kept their hands on policy. Many local companies, including Western Electric, Weston Instruments, and Singer, contributed about $335,000 in the form of equipment, facilities, and teachers. In 1967, the project enlisted more than 2,000 trainees, and industry people think the venture was successful. But some in Washington regard it as a failure because of the high dropout rate, about 50 percent.

At bottom was a basic disagreement about what the program ought to do and how. The government agencies, which did not always agree or work together, felt it should provide a broad fundamental education for the trainees, and argued that any trainee who entered the course should be duly graduated. Industry, however, felt that the program would generate motivation best by teaching the trainees useful skills as soon as possible, and by relating the academic work to their jobs. It wanted to teach the Three R's in only the first three weeks of the nine-week course, and then to proceed to shop math, blueprint reading, hand and shop tools, and so on. Although a high graduation rate would look good on government reports, industry argued that a graduation certificate should vouch for a student's ability to do good work.

"This scheme," says Paul W. Smith, director of industrial and labor relations for Western Electric and one of the founders of SEED, "was an effort to mobilize the business community. We realized that many companies would have to change their traditional methods of hiring; we made it clear that many of our trainees might not meet the usual high intelligence, dexterity, or physical standards that business has been accustomed to set up. Since we wanted companies to modify their practices, however, we had to be sure our certificates of graduation were evidence of the trainees' ability to perform." In other words, all the trainees were not equipped to become metalworkers, and it would do no good to pretend that they all were.

Industry also complained bitterly about the frustrations of dealing with various government agencies at once. "We had to get approval from one state and three Washington agencies for money, and this was time-consuming," says Smith. "In my opinion, no businessman has that kind of time."

The SEED affair doubtless provides only a foretaste of the problems business will encounter in hiring and training the unemployables. It is also bound to run into new and complex problems as government and Negro pressure mounts for "upward mobility"—i.e., for equal opportunity in promotion. But the problems are surmountable. Precisely because business has always been obliged to use human resources efficiently, it is demonstrating once again that unique ability to reclaim human resources by putting them to productive use.

4

MORE DOLLARS
AND
MORE DIPLOMAS

by Edmund K. Faltermayer

There has been so much authentic bad news about the condition of American Negroes, and so much guilt about the bad news among American whites, that it is often hard to get a hearing for some remarkably good news. Much of it is in the form of government data: it has come in slowly and been reported piecemeal. It has, accordingly, done very little to offset the gloom enveloping the monstrous human problems of the slums, where attention has been riveted and where good news is indeed hard to find. But Negroes have been steadily moving out of the slums, and nowadays only about a third of northern Negroes still live there—a fact that may come as a stunning surprise to most Americans. By several other indicators, furthermore, the gap between Negroes and whites is being narrowed; and by just about all indicators, Negroes are far better off today than they were in the recent past. Their children are staying in school longer, their incomes are rising rapidly, and more of them are getting relatively high-status jobs formerly closed to them.

What the statistics show, says Herman P. Miller of the U.S. Census Bureau, is that "most Negro men and women are succeeding against overwhelming odds." The data make clear that most Negroes want to be in the country's main-stream. More important, they demonstrate that Negroes have the *ability* to get into the mainstream.

The most important barometer of Negro progress is income, or "green power" as some Negro leaders like to call it, and here the trend is definitely up. Between 1960 and 1966 the median annual income of non-white families, as measured in constant 1966 dollars, increased by roughly one-third, to about $4,600.* Since the median figure for white families rose by only one-fifth during this period, to about $7,700, Negro income as a proportion of white income advanced from 55 percent to 60 percent. At the same time, the proportion of Negro families below the poverty line has declined considerably. As recently as 1959, half the country's non-white families lived below the line as it is currently defined by the federal government. (For a nonfarm family of four, with two children, the line is drawn at $3,300 a year.) By 1966 the ratio was down to 35 percent. Meanwhile, as the chart on page 80 shows, well-to-do Negro families—those with incomes exceeding $7,000 a year—came to constitute almost 30 percent of the total.

With 11 percent of the country's population, Negroes still have only 6 or 7 percent of the aggregate money income, FOR-TUNE estimates. However, this works out to some $30 billion a year before taxes—enough for Negroes to be taken seriously by corporate marketing executives. In certain consumer mar-

---

* *Much of the available government statistical data refers not to Negroes as such, but to "non-whites," a category that includes Indians and Americans of Asian origin as well as Negroes. But since Negroes represent 92 percent of the non-white population, data on non-whites fairly accurately reflect their condition. The terms Negro and non-white are used interchangeably in this article and in the charts on the following pages.*

kets, e.g., for clothing, they spend more heavily than whites with comparable incomes; and especially in some of the big-city areas where they are increasingly concentrated, they represent a major new market.

The majority of Negroes increasingly are displaying respect for many of the traditional middle-class virtues, too. Until recently, for example, the weak position of the male in the "matriarchal" Negro society had seemed self-perpetuating, in part because the girls typically completed more years of schooling than the boys. In the short period from 1960 to 1966, however, this situation has been reversed. Today the median number of years of school completed by non-white males in the twenty-five to twenty-nine age bracket is 12.1, compared to 11.9 for girls. In the same short period, moreover, non-white males have narrowed the education gap between themselves and white males; the difference in median years of schooling completed is down from nearly two years to only a half-year.

While they are still viewed as unambitious by many whites, most Negroes, even those who live in the worst slums where their incentives have supposedly been dulled by welfare payments, are quite capable of displaying old-fashioned American gumption. When Ford Motor Co. announced in October that it intended to hire 6,500 of the hard-core unemployed in the Detroit area, 14,000 persons swamped the special offices set up in poor neighborhoods. Over 4 percent of the country's employed Negroes—not much less than the proportion of whites —hold two or more jobs. A typical moonlighter is Ralph Earl Johnson, who works nights making automobile drive shafts at one of Chrysler's Detroit plants and has lately begun to drive a taxi by day, boosting his take-home pay to $200 a week. Says Johnson, a high-school graduate with a wife and two small children: "If a Negro wants to make it, he can make it."

The problems of the Negro family are well known and certainly severe. The proportion of non-white babies born out of wedlock is still rising, to 26 percent in 1965 (versus 4 percent for whites), and the proportion of non-white families headed by females has risen further in recent years, to 23.7 percent (versus 9 percent for whites). For a disturbingly large number of Negroes, obviously, the family is every bit as unstable an institution as it was said to be three years ago in the controversial Labor Department report entitled *The Negro Family,* written by Daniel P. Moynihan. Nevertheless, some of the figures aren't as bad as they look. For example, the reason the proportion of illegitimate Negro children is rising is not that the "illegitimate birth rate" is rising. Actually, it has declined slightly in recent years—but the "legitimate birth rate" is falling faster. Illegitimacy is concentrated heavily among the poorest slum Negroes.

Children without fathers seem more a class than a racial phenomenon. In any case, the differences between Negroes and whites in this respect are not so great when the families being contrasted are in the same income brackets. Census data for 1959 (the most recent figures available) show that, among Negro families with an annual income of $2,000 or less, only 59 percent of children lived with both parents; for white children at the same income level the figure was 69 percent. In families with incomes between $2,000 and $4,000, the proportions were much higher in both cases—82 percent for non-white children, versus 88 percent for whites; and in the $8,000-and-over category the nonwhite proportion was 95 percent, versus 99 percent for whites. The heritage of slavery notwithstanding, the fact is that the majority of Negro families remain together as a functioning unit.

The most notable achievement of Negroes in recent years, by far, has been the winning of more and better jobs. To be sure, the non-white unemployment rate continues to be high, touching 8.8 percent in the fourth quarter of 1967, versus 3.8 percent for whites. Nevertheless, the basic trend is encouraging, particularly when viewed against the background of the doomsaying of the early 1960's.

At that time, employment prospects for a typical Negro entering the labor market looked exceedingly dismal. Less educated than his white counterpart, he was forced to compete primarily for manual and unskilled jobs, which, in the view of many economists at the time, were disappearing under the impact of "automation." Simultaneously, the number of Negro job seekers was rising rapidly: between 1961 and 1966, as it turned out, the non-white civilian labor force grew by 700,000; and because another 324,000 non-whites moved off the farm in those years, the total number of non-whites seeking civilian *nonfarm* jobs grew by more than a million. In view of the sluggish growth rates of the U.S. economy in the late 1950's and early 1960's, and the wide publicity given to automation, those who forecast that the urban economy could absorb so many additional Negroes were generally written off as hopeless optimists.

The U.S. economy, however, began to grow faster in the early 1960's. As a result, enough new jobs were created to absorb not only that one-million-plus increase in the non-white urban labor force, but an additional 300,000 Negroes as well. In the process, the non-white unemployment rate, which had stood at 12.4 percent in 1961, dropped to 7.3 percent in 1966 and early 1967 before turning up again toward the end of the year. Significantly, the nearly 1,370,000 new non-agricultural jobs that were filled by non-whites included more than 650,000 blue-collar jobs in the semiskilled, unskilled, and service categories that are most vulnerable to automation. Indeed, it is now clear that the disappearance of such jobs in the late 1950's was due less to mechanization per se than to the fact that the U.S. economy had been growing slowly, and the number of new manual jobs opening up to Negroes barely exceeded the number displaced by machines.

Even more noteworthy, however, have been the recent Negro gains at the upper end of the occupational ladder— i.e., in winning more and more of the white-collar and skilled blue-collar jobs that are less vulnerable to displacement by machines and that are increasing faster than jobs in general. Between 1961 and 1966, when total non-white employment was increasing by 14.9 percent, the number of white-collar jobs held by Negroes grew by 45.9 percent, and the number of skilled blue-collar jobs in the better-paid "craftsmen and foremen" category increased by 41.8 percent. As recently as ten years ago, only 17 percent of employed Negroes were in these higher-status white- and blue-collar occupations; by 1966 the proportion exceeded 28 percent.

Negroes are also increasing their share of the very best white-collar jobs. In 1956, for example, non-whites accounted for 10.3 percent of total employment but held only 3.7 percent of the professional and technical jobs. Ten years later, their share of such jobs had increased to 5.9 percent.

As the Negro professional class grows in size, it is also changing in composition. For years, Negro professionals were overwhelmingly concentrated in fields that served their own race, especially medicine, law, and the ministry; but they

Text continued on page 86

Overleaf, a statistical primer

Nearly half of U.S. Negroes now live outside the South, mainly in central cities.

In 1940, as the bar charts (left) show, 77 percent of American Negroes lived in the South, but this was on the eve of a wartime industrial expansion that sparked a heavy migration to other parts of the country. By 1966, the proportion had shrunk to only 55 percent. The detailed breakdown for 1966 shows that nearly three-quarters of the Negroes outside the South live in the core cities of metropolitan areas. But only about a third of those northern city dwellers—or about a tenth of the total U.S. Negro population—live in areas of concentrated poverty, i.e. the bad slum neighborhoods where most of the rioting has erupted.

The charts below show that Negroes are moving steadily into white-collar occupations—professional, managerial, clerical, and sales jobs—and into the more skilled blue-collar jobs, as craftsmen and foremen. As recently as 1961, only 4.1 percent of the country's professional and technical jobs were held by Negroes (below, left); by 1966, the figure was up to 5.9 percent. But Negroes are still underrepresented in the better jobs. As the chart (below, right) shows, only 28 percent of employed Negroes have the jobs generally identified with higher status—compared with nearly two-thirds of the country's whites.

Negro population:

12,900,000 — 1940
U.S. excluding South
South

15,000,000 — 1950

18,800,000 — 1960

21,500,000 — 1966

Poverty areas
Metropolitan areas
Other city areas
Suburbs
Small towns and farms

Poverty areas
Metropolitan areas
Other city areas
Suburbs
Small towns and farms

They are getting more of the better jobs . . .

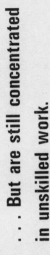

Negro representation in different job categories

Occupation	1940	1956	1961	1966
Higher status				
Professional and technical	3.7%	3.7%	4.1%	5.9%
Managers, officials, proprietors	1.7	2.2	2.4	2.8
Clerical	1.2	3.8	5.4	6.3
Sales		1.8	2.5	3.1
Craftsmen and foremen	2.7	4.2	4.9	6.3
Lower status				
Semiskilled	5.8	11.3	11.9	12.9
Laborers	21.0	26.8	25.7	25.3
Household service	22.4	46.6	43.4	41.8
Other service workers	11.8	21.3	20.1	21.0
Farmers and farm managers	15.2	8.5	7.4	6.1
Farm laborers and foremen	17.5	22.9	24.8	20.2

. . . But are still concentrated in unskilled work.

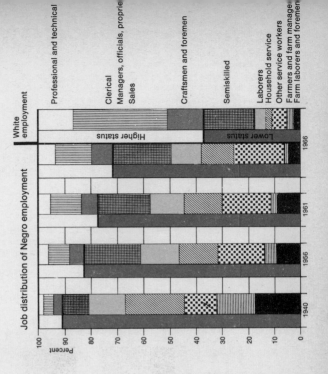

Job distribution of Negro employment

Higher status

- Professional and technical
- Clerical
- Managers, officials, proprietors
- Sales
- Craftsmen and foremen

Lower status

- Semiskilled
- Laborers
- Household service
- Other service workers
- Farmers and farm managers
- Farm laborers and foremen

White employment

1966 1961 1956 1940

Percent: 100 90 80 70 60 50 40 30 20 10 0

More Negroes are reaching the middle-income brackets, and fewer live in poverty . . .

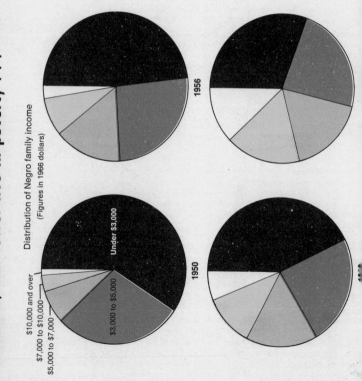

Distribution of Negro family income
(Figures in 1966 dollars)

$10,000 and over
$7,000 to $10,000
$5,000 to $7,000
$3,000 to $5,000
Under $3,000

1950

1956

Back in 1950, a mere 1.6 percent of the country's Negro families had annual incomes of $10,000 or more (measured in 1966 dollars). Since then, as the charts at the left show, the proportion has increased dramatically, to 12.2 percent in 1966—about one-eighth of all Negro families. The proportion of all Negro families with incomes above $7,000 has climbed from only 5 percent to 29 percent during this same sixteen-year period. (Outside the South, about 40 percent of Negro families had over $7,000 in 1966.)

Despite those substantial increases in income, Negroes have gained very little relative to whites since 1953. The two charts below at left, based on data compiled especially for For-TUNE by the Bureau of the Census, make it clear that Negro and white median incomes have both been rising at about the same rates over the period as a whole. However, the chart at the right, below, shows that, for the U.S. considered as a whole, median Negro income is somewhat higher in relation to white income than it was in 1953. The explanation of this seeming paradox is continuing migration from the South (where Negroes lag further behind whites) to the rest of the U.S. (where the relative income gap is smaller).

. . . But the gap between Negro and white incomes
has narrowed only slightly.

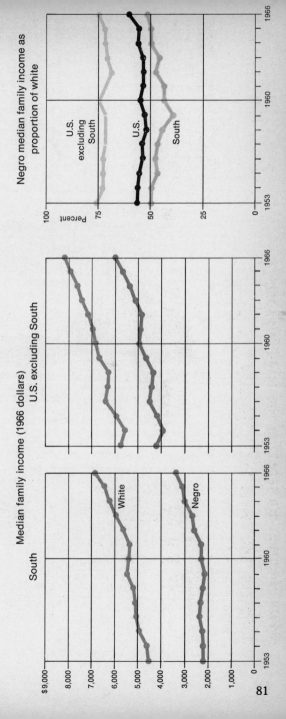

Median family income (1966 dollars)

South

U.S. excluding South

Negro median family income as proportion of white

The unemployment rate for Negroes
is higher than for whites . . .

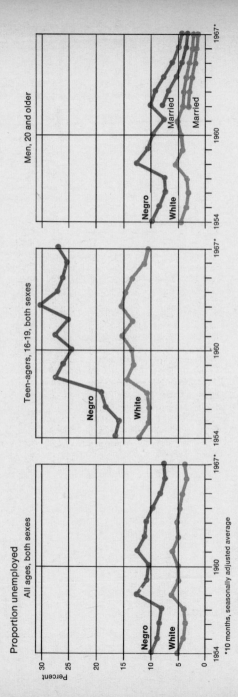

Proportion unemployed
All ages, both sexes

Teen-agers, 16-19, both sexes

Men, 20 and older

*10 months, seasonally adjusted average

In recent years, during booms as well as recessions, the unemployment rate has consistently been about twice as high for Negroes as for whites. Among teen-agers the spread in rates has actually widened over the years. But unemployment is relatively low among Negro men over twenty, especially those who are married. (Data for married men are available only since 1962.)

Negro unemployment is worst of all in the slums. The data charted below, from the worst Negro slums in six cities, show all those the Labor Department calls "sub-employed," i.e., the unemployed, part-time workers, those working full time but at low wages, half of the able-bodied men not seeking work, and half of an assumed "undercount" of adult men probably missed in the surveys.

. . . And the problem is worst in the slums.

"Sub-employment" rates in slum areas surveyed in November, 1966

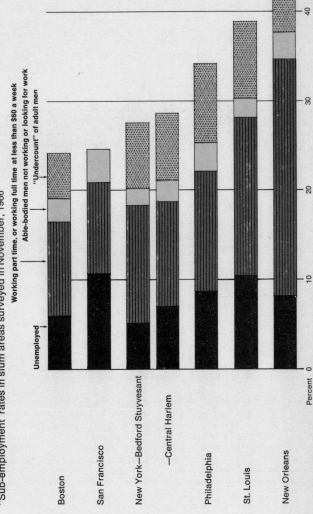

Working part time, or working full time at less than $60 a week

Able-bodied men not working or looking for work

"Undercount" of adult men

Unemployed

Boston
San Francisco
New York—Bedford Stuyvesant
—Central Harlem
Philadelphia
St. Louis
New Orleans

Percent

Negroes are getting more years of schooling.

As recently as 1958, two-thirds of young Negroes dropped out of high school without finishing; today, more than half are sticking it out until the twelfth grade. Census Bureau data (right) indicate that the gap in median years of schooling between young Negro and white men has been narrowing rapidly, from two years in 1961 to only a half-year in 1966. Moreover, young Negro men now stay in school longer than Negro girls, reversing a long-standing pattern. Though Negroes are gaining on whites in "quantity" of education, the quality of their education still lags seriously (chart below). On a standardized test of reading and other subjects, made in 1965 as part of a study for the Department of Health, Education, and Welfare, twelfth-grade Negroes achieved only ninth-grade scores, on the average.

Meanwhile, as other data from H.E.W. make clear (bottom), Negroes have been moving closer to whites over the years in life expectancy at birth.

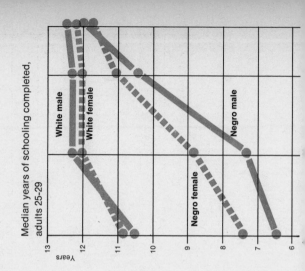

Median years of schooling completed, adults 25-29

Actual grade in school:	Test grade level		The "gap"
	Negro	White	
Sixth	4.4	6.8	2.4
Ninth	7.0	9.9	2.9
Twelfth	9.2	12.7	3.5

They are also living longer, and gaining on whites in longevity.

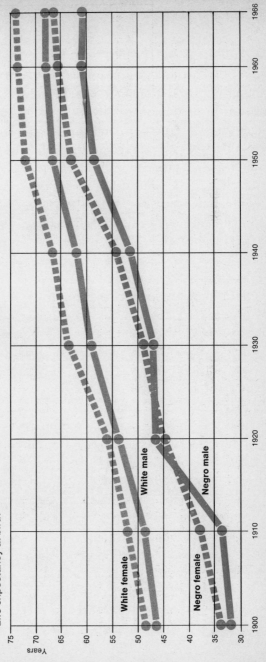

Life expectancy at birth

Years

White female

White male

Negro female

Negro male

1900 | 1910 | 1920 | 1930 | 1940 | 1950 | 1960 | 1966

30 | 35 | 40 | 45 | 50 | 55 | 60 | 65 | 70 | 75

have recently begun moving into direct competition with whites in "mainstream" professions. Between 1950 and 1960 the number of Negro architects increased by 72 percent, the number of natural scientists by 77 percent, and the number of engineers by 200 percent, and this trend has continued during the 1960's. Corporate recruiters, who five years ago rarely visited Negro colleges and universities, now descend in droves upon such leading institutions as Howard, Morehouse, and Fisk, and are especially eager to hire Negro engineers.

In some fields, such as entertainment and sports, Negroes have had a good share of the jobs for a decade or more. (About 20 percent of all players in the National Football League nowadays are Negroes.) And Negroes are rapidly moving toward complete equality in the military services. Vietnam is the first conflict in which all American military units have fought on a fully integrated basis; over 5 percent of the majors in the U.S. Army, and more than a sixth of the platoon sergeants, are now Negroes. With considerable success, the Defense Department has recently been pressing for open housing in privately owned apartments and houses near military bases, and the department's efforts promise to make military careers even more attractive to non-whites in the future.

Negroes are still a long way from occupational parity, to be sure. If they were represented in all occupations in proportion to their share of the population, they would today have one-ninth of the jobs in each category. Despite the recent gains, they still are underrepresented in nearly all the higher-status jobs and concentrated in unskilled and menial occupations. Over one-fourth of the unskilled laborers in industry and of the country's service workers are still non-white. Nevertheless, the direction of events is clear: despite their lower average level of education, Negroes are moving toward "parity," in an increasingly sophisticated labor market.

The upgrading that has taken place is especially striking when seen in a longer historical perspective. As recently as 1940, when 77 percent of the Negro population still lived in the South (compared to 55 percent at present), only one Negro in eleven—compared with one in three and a half today—had a white-collar or skilled blue-collar job. Except for a few semiskilled jobs in industry, the Negro labor force was largely restricted to subsistence-level farming and to various menial tasks in manufacturing and service.

The fact that more and more Negroes are now working side by side with whites in high-level occupations obviously does not mean that a large proportion of them will shortly be *living* side by side with whites, or that racial prejudice will soon disappear. Still, a reasonably workable biracial society may be possible in another generation or so. A good deal of what is commonly thought of as racial prejudice has less to do with race than with class; the animus is directed toward people mainly because of their occupations, grammar, and mode of dress. In the U.S., says Dorothy K. Newman of the Bureau of Labor Statistics, "as soon as people pick up the culture, the mode of speech, and the style of life of the majority, they are accepted." Mrs. Newman believes that Negroes already enjoy a higher status, at least so far as occupations are concerned, than Chinese- and Japanese-Americans did in 1930, when prejudice against Asians was still strong. "Who would have thought a generation ago," she asks, "that the Oriental would be accepted everywhere?"

"There is no question," says Whitney Young Jr., executive director of the National Urban League, "that the barriers to Negroes are crumbling and many have been removed altogether." Young and most other Negro leaders nevertheless view the statistics in a somber light. Negro gains look much less encouraging when they are matched against whites' gains. In unemployment the rate for Negroes remains much higher than for whites. Even the relatively low unemployment rate for married Negro men over twenty, which averaged 3.4 percent in the first ten months of 1967, is more than double the recent 1.6-percent rate for married white men.

Negro gains in income, it is true, have been more rapid than whites' gains recently. However, the long-term trend has not been so favorable. In 1952, during the Korean-War boom, median family income for non-whites climbed to 57 percent of the white figure. After a couple of dips and rises, it was only three percentage points higher in 1966. Even this gain largely reflects the movement of Negroes out of the South, where income levels are generally low. Relative gains *within* the South, and within the rest of the U.S., have been negligible. (See the chart on page 81.)

The median figures, of course, lump together Negroes who are advancing economically with those who are not. The reality seems to be that *some* Negroes, especially those in the middle and upper income brackets, are gaining rapidly on whites, while others, especially slum dwellers, are losing ground in relative terms. "What you are getting," says one Negro, familiar with the data, "is a stretching of the rope."

In the big northern cities, the slum dwellers now represent a minority of the Negro population. But the slum populations are still big enough, and the incomes of slum dwellers low enough, to drag down the average and median figures. In Watts, one of the poorest communities in the South Los Angeles area, the median income for Negro families, as measured in constant dollars, increased only about 4 percent between 1959 and 1964—far less than Negro or white incomes in general. In four Cleveland slum areas real incomes actually *declined* during the same period, by something like 10 percent. But the median income for *all* Cleveland Negroes increased in 1959-64 from $5,055 to $5,489, and in the more prosperous Negro neighborhoods the figure rose from $6,178 to $7,285. (The figures are in 1964 dollars.) Clearly, there has been a widening of the spread in incomes, and a widening of the gulf between the Negro have-nots and the haves.

The unemployment situation in the Negro slums, not surprisingly, is also worse than for Negroes in general. And the unemployment data tell only part of the story about the serious *under*employment in these neighborhoods. The Labor Department conducted a special study of what it calls "sub-employment" in a number of slum areas around the U.S. in November, 1966. The "sub-employed" include not only those looking for work and unable to find it—i.e., the unemployed—but also part-time workers seeking full-time jobs, and full-time workers earning what the Labor Department defines as subminimum wages (less than $60 a week in the case of the head of a household under sixty-five years of age and less than $56 a week in the case of any other wage earners in the household under sixty-five). The sub-employed also include half the adult males not in the labor force; the presumption is that they would be out looking for a job if they hadn't given up hope of finding one. Finally, the sub-employed include half the adult males estimated to have been missed in the survey.*

---

* Some persons are, of course, missed in all employment surveys. But the "undercount" is especially high in slum areas, particularly among Negro men in the twenty-to-thirty-nine-year age bracket. Even in the last decennial census in 1960, Census Bureau officials believe, about 9 percent of the Negro population was missed.

In the slums of North Philadelphia, 11 percent of the labor force was counted as unemployed in November, 1966, which is bad enough; but the sub-employment rate was 34.2 percent. In the other Negro slum areas surveyed, sub-employment ranged from 24.2 percent (Boston) to 45.3 percent (New Orleans). The sub-employment figures, admittedly, are based upon some fairly arbitrary statistical procedures and assumptions. Furthermore, the total numbers involved are not unmanageable. A sampling of the Bureau of Labor Statistics in September, 1966, suggested that the total number (i.e., including some outside the slums) of Negroes sixteen years of age and older who had withdrawn from the labor force because they were "discouraged" was only about 175,000. Unemployment among Negro teen-agers is not quite as bad as it looks, either, since about a third of the Negro teen-agers listed as unemployed are in school and looking only for *part-time* work. And the number of non-white teen-agers who have dropped out of school and have been unable to find work averaged only 124,000 for the whole country during the first six months of 1967. Nevertheless, the basic point of the sub-employment concept is valid: the situation within the slums is indeed a good deal worse than the usual data indicate.

But even the "haves" among the Negroes can be discouraged if they view progress in relative terms. Most of the gains in white-collar employment have been confined to government jobs. Almost 60 percent of the postal workers in Los Angeles are non-white, for example, as are 35 percent of Detroit's schoolteachers. Barriers in the private sector are beginning to drop, but Negro representation in the business world is still relatively small. And it is virtually nonexistent so far as the top jobs are concerned.

Perhaps more disturbing is the scarcity of companies owned and operated by Negro entrepreneurs. In 1966, Negroes still represented only 2.8 percent of the country's "managers, officials, and proprietors," and a good many of them were working in government or for white-controlled companies. This situation deeply worries such men as Berkeley G. Burrell, president of the National Business League, an organization founded in 1900 by Booker T. Washington. There is an urgent need, Burrell contends, for more Negro-run enterprises, whose chiefs could use their positions to influence community affairs and local politics.

For most better-off Negroes, the biggest relative discrepancies continue to show up in the figures on education and housing. While young Negroes now spend almost as much time in schools as whites do, they lag far behind whites in the *quality* of their education. The seriousness of the gap is evident in the results of a standardized test of reading and other subjects, given in 1965 in connection with a study of Negro and white educational opportunity by James S. Coleman of Johns Hopkins University for the Department of Health, Education and Welfare. Twelfth-grade Negroes could achieve only ninth-grade scores, on the average, placing them the equivalent of three-and-a-half school years behind their white counterparts. The Coleman report observed, however, that the academic differential was related to social rather than racial differences; Negroes and whites of the same social class did about equally well.

Unequal educational opportunity is due in large measure to housing segregation. Around the country, the last few years have seen the emergence of a few genuinely integrated communities—i.e., communities that are not merely in the process of becoming all-black but have fair prospects of maintaining a mixture of the two races. Two examples, West Mount Airy in Philadelphia, and the Hyde Park-Kenwood area of Chicago, prove that whites and blacks can live together, and undoubtedly represent a preview of what could become commonplace in another generation. In both instances new white families are moving in to replace those that leave, property values have risen, and in the case of West Mount Airy the proportion of white pupils in the local elementary school has become stabilized at about 30 percent in the last few years. (Though the population is about three-quarters white, the proportion of whites in the school is lower because many of the community's white children attend private and parochial schools, while a sizable number of Negro children from adjoining communities swell the non-white enrollment.)

To be sure, there are some special reasons for the stability of these communities. The Negroes of West Mount Airy are fairly affluent, many of them professionals—the types with the best chance for fitting into a predominantly white, middle-class milieu; while the whites, who also enjoy above-average incomes, are strongly attached to the area because it is very attractive and offers fast commuting to downtown by rail transit. The burgeoning University of Chicago complex, similarly, helps to anchor a sizable and growing white population to the Hyde Park-Kenwood area. Truly integrated neighborhoods are still rare, and they are nearly all, like these two, within the central cities. The suburbs, meanwhile, remain overwhelmingly white.

Negroes are beginning to move to the suburbs in some metropolitan areas. In suburban Westchester County, north of New York City, the Negro population shot up by 19.2 percent between 1960 and 1965—compared to a 4.4 percent increase for whites—and the Negro proportion of the county's total population increased to 8.4 percent. In the Chicago area, Negroes made up barely 3 percent of the suburban population in 1960 but, according to estimates by Pierre de Visé of De Paul University, they accounted for more than 9 percent of total suburban population growth between 1960 and 1965.

But the Negroes' recent gains in suburbia have been concentrated in towns that already had sizable Negro neighborhoods, such as Mount Vernon and White Plains in Westchester County and Evanston and Maywood near Chicago; the majority of suburban towns have experienced hardly any Negro influx at all. Only here and there are Negroes beginning to crack some hitherto all-white suburbs. During the last two years, fifteen Chicago suburbs received their first Negro families; and Park Forest, that symbol of the young new middle-class way of life described in great detail in William H. Whyte's *The Organization Man,* now has nearly a hundred Negro families out of a total of 8,022.

The current movement of Negroes to the suburbs, moreover, is still far too slow to alter the larger trend toward blacker central cities surrounded by a ring of white suburbs. Nationwide, the Negro population of suburban areas increased by an average of only 37,000 a year between 1960 and 1966. And because *all* of the white-population growth in the country's metropolitan areas occurred in the suburbs during this period, the Negro proportion of the suburban population actually *declined,* from 4.6 percent to 4.1 percent. Meanwhile in the central cities, which suffered a slight decrease in white population and an enormous rise in the Negro population, the proportion of Negroes increased from 17 to 20 percent. In the bigger core cities the proportion went much higher, reaching 66 percent in Washington, D.C., about 50 percent in

Newark, 36 percent in St. Louis, and 34 percent in Detroit and in Cleveland.

These statistics tell a good deal about what needs to be done by government and business to speed Negro progress. They suggest, for example, that ways must be found to move more Negro families into the suburbs. The purpose should not be to prevent some of the core cities from becoming predominantly black—this may happen anyway, and need not be a calamity—but to scatter *enough* non-whites in outlying communities so that Negroes no longer think of the suburbs as virtually off-limits to them.

More than half of American Negroes are still concentrated in the South. In recent years the northward Negro migration has slowed somewhat; indeed, a few northern cities, such as Detroit, have had no net influx for several years. But the migration might easily speed up again, and might create unmanageable new assimilation problems for some northern and western cities, if the Negro's lot improves more slowly in the South than in the rest of the country.

Rural Negroes in recent years have been migrating heavily into southern cities, and they represent a potent new force in these cities' politics. Atlanta's population, for example, is now 44 percent Negro, and New Orleans is not far behind with 41 percent. One big benefit has been a dramatic improvement in Negroes' employment opportunities in local government. In 1963 all of Atlanta's refuse collectors were black, while the men who drove the sanitation trucks were all white. But prodding by the Urban League, combined with a new appreciation for the Negro vote in city hall, has brought about a change. In recent months, more than half the persons hired for municipal jobs have been Negroes and, important from a symbolic standpoint, *some* of those sanitation truck drivers are now black, and some of the men loading the trucks are white.

Dr. Vivian Henderson, president of Clark College and a leading Negro economist, believes the South may offer the best opportunities for Negroes in the years to come because Negroes constitute an even larger proportion of the population in big southern cities than they do in most northern metropolises. Atlanta is expected to be more than 50 percent black by the early 1970's, Henderson notes. He adds: "Once the Negroes become the majority group in Atlanta, a lot of them will say 'There's no use in our running to New York.'"

Meanwhile, Negroes still lag further behind whites in the South than anywhere else in the U.S. This is especially true in private industry, where the segregation of jobs between Negroes and whites is still widespread. This pattern is beginning to break down under the influence of the federal government's new Equal Employment Opportunity Commission; besides, many companies are subject to nondiscrimination provisions in federal contracts.

The chief problem is no longer the unskilled Negro just off the southern farm; all but 6 percent of U.S. Negroes have already abandoned farming as an occupation. Rather, it is the Southern Negro who has got out of farming but still resides in a rural area or small town. Nearly a quarter of the country's Negroes live in such areas in the South, and many of them will be pouring into both southern and northern metropolitan regions in the years ahead if they cannot find work where they live. If this movement is to be manageable, more companies, particularly in such industries as textiles, where jobs are scattered through small towns, will have to intensify their efforts to hire and train Negro workers.

5

THE ST. LOUIS ECONOMIC BLUES

by William S. Rukeyser

The plight of the Negro poor is intertwined with a momentous change that has taken place in the economic functions of cities. Innovations in technology, transportation, and communication have undermined the traditional bases of urban economies. This undermining has weakened the cities' ability to provide industrial jobs, and to cope with the costs that the presence of the poor imposes. The nature of the change can be seen with special clarity in St. Louis.

For more than a century, St. Louis' North Side has been the locale of the poor. Generations of immigrants—Irish, Germans, Italians, Russians, Poles—have crowded its dingy streets, raised children in its bleak tenements and row-houses and ultimately, as their lot improved, moved out.

Today the North Side (or more precisely, the Near North Side) is inhabited overwhelmingly by Negroes, immigrants from the worn-out farms of the American South. Their conditions—poverty, crime, widespread illiteracy, disease, high infant mortality—are not much different from those of their predecessors, but their chances of following the old routes out of the North Side are radically worse. Racial discrimination dims their prospects, of course; but perhaps even more significant is that the Negroes' predominance on the North Side has coincided with a far-reaching economic shuffle that has crippled St. Louis' ability to put them to work.

The situation is blurred by statistics that lump together growing and declining sections of the metropolitan area. For example, manufacturing employment in the St. Louis metropolitan area rose about 5 percent between 1959 and 1965. But this figure embraces two opposite trends. In St. Louis County over that span of years, manufacturing employment rose 42 percent; in the city, it *declined* 6 percent.

The contrast between core and hinterland is unusually pronounced in the St. Louis area because that city's boundaries were permanently fixed a long time ago. St. Louis has been fenced in, restricted to its current sixty-two square miles, ever since 1876, when the city shortsightedly cut itself free from the adjoining 497 square miles of St. Louis County. Back then, St. Louis had small reason to fear the consequences of going it alone. The city had been thriving since the days when its warehouses outfitted the pioneers, and its location on the Mississippi River seemed to guarantee its continued economic vitality. ("St. Louis," says a local real-estate developer, "was a well-developed commercial center when Chicago was a cow pasture.")

Through most of its history, St. Louis County was quiet, thinly populated territory, economically dependent on the city. But in the years since World War II the county has outstripped the city in population, taken over the metropolitan area's fastest-growing industries, and built its busiest new shopping centers. The county seat, Clayton, has even become competitive with downtown St. Louis as a site for high-rise office buildings and apartments.

A quarter of a million people, virtually all of them whites, have moved out of St. Louis since 1950. Even with a large increase in the number of Negro residents over those seventeen years, the city's population has shrunk from 857,000 to under 700,000. By January, 1968, almost two out of five St. Louisans were Negroes, more than double the 1950 proportion. The whites who have moved out have included a large share of the city's better-educated and more prosperous people. The Negroes who have moved in have been generally ill-educated and poor.

Despite the population decline, a visitor to the central business district near the Mississippi River might conclude that St. Louis remains as economically vibrant as ever. The infusion of half a billion dollars of public and private money has transformed some of the more depressing downtown areas over the last decade. Along streets where grimy loft buildings and senile hotels once caused passing businessmen to yearn for suburbia, glassy office and apartment towers now cluster near Eero Saarinen's Gateway Arch and the new $29-million Busch Stadium. Recent additions to the skyline include a cylindrical riverfront hotel, a balconied office building, and the concrete shell of Pet Inc.'s new fifteen-story national headquarters.

Even away from the river, St. Louis still has the look and feel of a working town. Its factories churn out a myriad of goods ranging from potato chips to artillery shells. A two-story General Motors plant stretching for three blocks along Union Boulevard assembles more Chevrolets than any other facility in the world. On the South Side's Pestalozzi Street, the pungent odors of beer-making still waft from the massive red-brick headquarters plant of the nation's largest brewer, Anheuser-Busch.

But the office buildings provide few jobs for the unskilled, and the big factories are less numerous than they used to be. Since the early 1950's, manufacturing employment in the city has declined by about one-quarter. Many former manufacturing plants stand vacant, forlornly decaying.

The decline of industry in the city has been a bitter development for the North Side, where a survey found unemployment running above 12 percent late in 1966. Expanding employment in the county has provided relatively few jobs for city dwellers. At its huge plant seventeen miles from the North Side, McDonnell Douglas, by far the biggest employer in the metropolitan area, has actively recruited and trained St. Louis Negroes. But though McDonnell's work force has swelled from 22,000 to 42,000 since 1960, the company still employs fewer than 5,000 St. Louisans. The proportion of city residents on the payroll has actually slumped since 1960, from 17 to 12 percent.

One employment obstacle for North Side people is the lack of direct public transportation to where the suburban jobs are. It takes as much as two hours, and three buses, to get from the North Side to the McDonnell plant. With the help of a federal grant, the city planned to start a direct bus service in 1968, probably from the North Side to the McDonnell area. But the number of industrial jobs out there for unskilled and semiskilled city people is much smaller than the number of unemployed North Siders. Scattered around in the suburbs are quite a few service jobs that North Siders could fill, but the wages are generally not high enough to make up for the long trip.

For North Siders, the drop in city industrial jobs has not been offset by an expansion of other employment in the city. In the kinds of jobs accessible to them, the picture is grim. For example, some 7,600 positions in retail and wholesale trade evaporated between 1959 and 1966 as competition from the suburbs cut sales in St. Louis; retail sales declined by around 10 percent during those years.

The national trend toward white-collar employment and away from unskilled and semiskilled industrial jobs is even more evident in the older cities than in the rest of the country. Yet because low-income families can normally command only the most obsolete, undesirable housing, they must continue to live in cities. The incongruous result is that white-collar jobs for suburbanites become more plentiful in cities while jobs for unskilled and semiskilled city dwellers become scarcer. Unemployed St. Louis Negroes can mull the paradox as they watch the rush-hour commuter jams on the Mark Twain Expressway, which skirts the North Side slums on its way to St. Louis County.

St. Louis' leaders believe it is evident that their problems demand a reuniting of city and county, and they seem impatient with the coolness of voters, particularly those in the suburbs, toward the idea. "Before we can really go forward as we should," says Raymond R. Tucker, a former mayor of St. Louis, "we need metropolitan, regional government in the area. The interests of the county and the city are not basically opposed. They are identical."

Few suburbanites see it that way. Many enjoy boasting that they rarely have any call to go to the city any more. To them, the interests of the city and the county seem not identical but opposed. They want their borders carefully sealed against any importation of St. Louis' social and economic maladies. Samuel Bernstein, head of the city's business development commission, complains, "There seems to be a Mason-Dixon line—and at times a Maginot line—between the city and county."

On its own, St. Louis does not have the resources to cope with the problems of the North Side and other poor areas. Median family income in St. Louis County is about 40 percent higher than in St. Louis, but while the city government collected an average of $254 annually from its residents through taxes and other charges in fiscal 1966, the per capita tax bill in the county was only $153. Despite its smaller tax bite, the county had sufficient funds to outspend the city by a wide margin on schools—$117 per capita against the city's $86.

Skimping on education is a recipe for perpetuating poverty, but St. Louis has little choice. Its revenues, hard-won through tax rates that provide one more reason for businesses to leave town, are disproportionately committed to a whole range of public services linked to poverty, crime, and dilapidation. On health and hospitals, for example, the city spent $34 per capita in 1966, the county $8. For police protection the figures were $32 and $10; for fire protection, $13 and $6.

Far from using its powers to ease the city's financial squeeze, the Missouri state government worsens it. A recent study carried out for the city government indicated that Missouri gets almost a quarter of its revenues from St. Louis, but that only about one-eighth of state expenditures flow back to the city. So the city increasingly relies on the federal government for help. Federal outlays in St. Louis run in the vicinity of $575 million a year.

St. Louis is doing everything it can think of to reverse the decline of industry. To encourage companies considering a St. Louis location, the city government offers advice on sites and, often, generous tax abatements. In December, 1967, the Board of Aldermen established an industrial-expansion authority with power to issue tax-exempt bonds and condemn blighted property for industrial sites.

However, it is almost certainly futile for St. Louis, or any major city, to base its hopes for the future on attracting a lot of large factories. The city government, sensibly, is relying on its incentives chiefly to keep existing businesses from leaving. To many manufacturers, including some of the biggest employers, the benefits of being adjacent to a large pool of untrained labor are questionable, while the efficiency of operating spread-out one-story factories on suburban acreage is clear. Furthermore, the city's traditional assets of central location and access to rail and river transportation have been devalued by superhighways and electronic communications.

In the long run, St. Louis may come to view the retreat of noisy factories and fuming trailer-trucks as a disguised boon. The city already has strengths as a center of office employment and recreational and cultural activities. Building on these strengths might provide a more promising channel for municipal energies than competing with the suburbs for industrial plants. By working to make itself a more attractive environment for middle-class people, as well as for non-industrial enterprises, the city might begin to lure back some of the people whose move to the suburbs has been a reluctant reaction to urban blight. Their return would stimulate retail trade and service industries, and fortify the cultural life of the city too.

The North Side, however, does not fit into this vision of a possible future. A continuing substitution of white-collar for blue-collar jobs does not promise any great widening of employment opportunities for North Side people. And their poverty hobbles the city. Welfare and other services to the poor drain away resources that the city could otherwise invest in public facilities and services to make itself a more appealing place for suburban people to visit, shop in, and perhaps even move to. St. Louis needs a decongestion of economic liabilities as well as an expansion of assets.

Many people who have thought about the matter, in St. Louis and elsewhere, would agree in a general way with the view expressed by Father Lucius Cervantes, a Jesuit sociologist and brother of St. Louis' present mayor. "The answer," he says, "is to disperse the ghetto. Jobs are in a ring around the city. Allow the poor to follow the jobs." Father Cervantes has some ideas, possibly a bit quixotic, on how that might be accomplished: "Scatter the sites of public housing. With rent subsidies, move a Negro family into one house in each block in the suburbs."

If a cross-migration could come about, with some middle-class whites moving back to the cities they work in and some Negroes moving out to the suburbs to live and work, it would be possible to discern a less clouded future for St. Louis—as well as a less crowded future for the Mark Twain Expressway. Perhaps this is the direction of hope, for St. Louis and other cities too. But nothing like this can be expected, on a scale large enough to matter, without some new political arrangements. The power of the city stops at that 1876 boundary, and the county beyond wants nothing less than an inflow of Negroes from the city.

Some overarching authority would be required to open up the suburbs to large numbers of Negroes—perhaps some kind of metropolitan government imposed, or at least fostered, by state intervention. It is not a good bet that effective new arrangements will emerge any time soon. Yet unless things move in that direction, it is hard to see any future for St. Louis—and by inference many other U.S. cities—except deepening economic blues.

6

THE CASE AGAINST THE UNIONS

by Thomas O'Hanlon

Moral ambiguity in the face of Negro demands for equality is present to some degree in all American institutions, but nowhere is the uneasiness more apparent than in the labor movement. In the past, unions have been catalysts of social change. They supported legislation to promote full employment and open housing. They invited Negro leaders to meetings to preach the virtues of a working-class coalition of Negroes and whites. And, in 1964, the A.F.L.-C.I.O. gave unequivocal support to the Civil Rights Act. However, when the act became law, the mood of brotherhood evaporated. Says former U.S. Assistant Attorney General John Doar, "Union concepts of security and seniority were formulated in the period of struggle between company and union. Now the struggle is between the Negroes and the unions."

At stake in the battle is white supremacy in broad areas of employment. Roughly two million of organized labor's 18 million members are Negroes. But they have been systematically excluded from some of the most powerful unions—e.g., in transportation and skilled trades—and most of the Negroes who are union members are concentrated in the least desirable jobs—the semiskilled trades, menial, or service occupations.

The lack of voluntary union compliance with the law and the coolness of many union leaders toward Negroes have galvanized the civil-rights organizations into a legal assault on all trade-union practices that smack of exclusion or discrimination. Since passage of the Civil Rights Act, the National Association for the Advancement of Colored People has filed over 700 complaints with federal agencies charging union discrimination. (Some 1,600 have been filed against employers and employment agencies.) Among practices under attack by the N.A.A.C.P. and, somewhat belatedly, by the Justice Department:

¶ The refusal of all but a few of the eighteen building-trades unions to open their ranks to qualified Negroes; most of the highly paid skilled construction jobs are held by whites.

¶ Industrial-union seniority systems that relegate Negroes to menial jobs. In many plants the senior Negro employees have less desirable jobs than the most junior of the whites.

¶ The systematic exclusion of Negroes from apprenticeship programs (mostly in the building trades); only 3 percent of registered apprentices are Negroes.

¶ Failure to eliminate locals that are confined to a single race. There are over 150 all-Negro A.F.L.-C.I.O. locals.

¶ The use of hiring halls and referral systems, to prevent qualified, nonunion Negroes from bidding for jobs.

¶ The deliberate exclusion of Negroes from unions in some industries.

¶ Union attempts to evade federal law by accepting a token number of Negroes.

The economic consequences of such discrimination cannot be accurately calculated, but they are obviously immense. Arthur M. Ross, Commissioner of the Bureau of Labor Statistics, analyzed a number of major trades in an attempt to determine statistically how many of those jobs ought to be held by Negroes. He concluded that if the percentage of the Negro work force employed in these trades was proportionate to white employment Negroes would then hold 37,000 more jobs as carpenters, 45,000 more as construction workers, 97,000 more as mechanics, 82,000 more as metal craftsmen, and 112,000 more as foremen.

Labor has not only failed to organize Negroes, but has failed to negotiate equal wages for those it has organized. Herman P. Miller, of the Bureau of the Census, estimates that on a national basis Negro factory hands earn 32 percent less than their white counterparts, while the wages of Negro truck drivers and delivery men are 42 percent below those received by whites. The pattern is similar in almost every industry. Dr. Vivian Henderson, president of Clark College, studied twenty-seven job categories in traditionally unionized industries *outside the South*. He found that in twenty-six of the twenty-seven categories non-whites earned substantially less than whites. (Bus drivers are the sole exception.)

It's true that some unions have taken affirmative action to eliminate racism and to help Negroes develop job skills. The Industrial Union Department of the A.F.L.-C.I.O. has helped form self-help community organizations in Watts, Newark, Philadelphia, and Chicago. The Operating Engineers and the Retail, Wholesale and Department Store Union, among others, have training programs to help Negroes move into higher-paying jobs. And the chief officers of the Transport Workers, the Packinghouse Workers, the American Federation of Teachers, and the United Auto Workers have consistently put pressure on locals to conform to the antidiscrimination clauses in their constitutions. The U.A.W., in fact, is the only international that has expelled a local for its racial practices. President Walter Reuther, strongly opposed to A.F.L.-C.I.O. inertia on a number of issues including civil rights, may yet lead the U.A.W. out of the federation.

However, the number of unions willing to take affirmative action against discrimination is pitifully small. The roots of bigotry are deepest in the building-trades and railroad unions. (The Brotherhood of Locomotive Firemen removed a "white only" clause from its constitution only a few years ago.) But discrimination is also widespread in many of the large industrial unions. Unions in the steel, paper, and tobacco industries, for instance, have made no attempt to eliminate clauses in collective-bargaining agreements that have the effect of favoring whites in layoffs and in promotion. And a substantial number of union leaders contend that unions are voluntary organizations that are obliged to conform only to the wishes of their members, not to the pressures of society.

While the A.F.L.-C.I.O. has expelled unions for corruption, it has never expelled a union for racial discrimination. All that the A.F.L.-C.I.O. constitution requires of its members is voluntary compliance with antidiscrimination statutes. Since affiliates of international unions have a great deal of autonomy, particularly in the craft and building trades, this doctrine of voluntaryism has failed.

Negroes believe that high-ranking labor officials simply do not understand the vital urgency of their demands. As Herbert Hill, labor director of the N.A.A.C.P., puts it: "Labor leaders are tragically incapable of understanding the dynamics of Negro protest. They express petulance and bitter resentment at increasing Negro demands and frequently are the most indignant because 'Negroes don't appreciate what we are doing.' " However, it is unfair to put all the blame on labor leaders. Many of them know that if they press hard to eliminate discrimination, they risk tearing apart their internationals because of resistance by the white rank and file.

In a way, it is a vicious circle: without strong leadership, white union members become apprehensive as Negroes move into the plant and then progress up the job scale. White employees—particularly recent immigrant ethnic groups—resist working under the supervision of a Negro. And in some jobs they even rebel against working alongside Negroes. (George Starling, president of Teamsters Local 100 in Cincinnati, asks, "Would you like to climb into a bunk that a nigger just got out of?") Moreover, the attitude of many union members toward Negroes cannot be divorced from the fear that as they get better jobs they may move next door.

For obvious reasons, everybody's best example of racial discrimination in the labor movement is provided by the highly paid building trades. Ever since the days of Samuel Gompers, the skilled trades of the A.F.L. have barred the door to Negroes. Such skilled craftsmen as plumbers, electricians, and sheet-metal workers enjoy the highest hourly wage rates in the nation. But while Negroes are employed as laborers and in the "trowel trades" as plasterers and bricklayers, they are frozen out of the highly paid job categories by union practices that bar entrance to apprenticeship programs.

The issue transcends union membership, important though that may be to a Negro plumber who works for $3.50 an hour maintaining a crumbling tenement, while his white counterpart makes up to $6.92 on construction projects. By barring Negroes from apprenticeship programs, the unions also effectively deny Negroes a chance to become entrepreneurs and building contractors. The majority of apprentices in the building trades expect to become supervisors and employers. A majority of electrical and plumbing firms in the country are operated by men with union cards.

Spokesmen for the construction unions insist that Negroes are not barred, but that most are incapable of qualifying for membership. "There are three groups of Negroes," explains A.F.L.-C.I.O. civil-rights director Donald Slaiman. "The middle-class families want their children to go to college. On the bottom are the dropouts, and they cannot qualify for the apprenticeship programs. The Negroes in between have three problems. They lack motivation. They are afraid of tests. They have an education gap."

The trouble with this sociological theory is that it is inaccurate. Indeed, a number of Negroes more highly qualified than George Meany himself (who holds a plumber's card) have been denied membership in unions. Take the case of Anderson L. Dobbins, who graduated from high school in Cincinnati with vocational training in electrical work, despite the advice of his instructor that the electrical industry in Cincinnati was closed to Negroes. In 1950, Dobbins entered Virginia's Hampton Institute and graduated five years later with a major in trade education and a minor in electricity. He then passed a test administered by the Electrical Underwriters in Newport News, Virginia, and in mid-1955 applied for membership to I.B.E.W. Local 212 in Cincinnati. He was rejected. Dobbins tried again in 1958, 1964, and 1965, and was barred each time.

Despite two suits filed by the N.A.A.C.P. and the Justice Department, Dobbins is still not a union member. "I can't do industrial work without a union card," says Dobbins. "In industrial work they make $6 an hour. But that's not the main thing. It also means more status. The work is more technical and you've got to be more on the ball. It gets you further on the road to being a master electrician. As a master electrician, you might earn $300 a week, be a foreman, or have your own shop." Dobbins' case is not unique. In 1966 the Ohio Civil Rights Commission found a "pattern of discrimination in the building-trades industry in Cincinnati, discernible among contractors, unions, and joint apprenticeship committees."

The power of the building-trades unions extends even to Washington. The Bureau of Apprenticeship and Training, an arm of the Labor Department, has been controlled by the construction unions since it was founded in 1937. Its present administrator is Hugh C. Murphy, a brother of the president of the Bricklayers. Until January, 1964, the bureau jogged along without enforcing antidiscrimination laws, but at that time Secretary of Labor Willard Wirtz ordered an end to discrimination in the selection of apprentices.

For three years many unions ignored the order and the bureau made no effort to enforce it. In the spring of 1967, Murphy was ordered to start de-registration proceedings against apprenticeship programs if the committee in charge did not sign a nondiscrimination agreement. Over a hundred have refused to comply. Indeed, Schoemann ordered his Plumbers' locals not to sign the pledge. "This has as much relationship to racial discrimination," says Schoemann, "as putting a man on the moon." Like most of his peers in the building trades, Schoemann insists that his union has the right to set up its own qualifications for apprentices. (The Plumbers, along with many other unions, now require applicants for apprenticeship to take written tests. See page 111.) The manpower administration of the Labor Department is demanding that apprenticeship committees actively seek minority candidates. But by early 1968 no apprenticeship program had been de-registered.

The first suit filed by the Justice Department against the building-trades unions, however, was an attack not on the apprenticeship programs but on that even more jealously guarded institution—the union hiring hall. In 1966 the Justice Department charged that the Building and Construction Trades Council of St. Louis, A.F.L.-C.I.O., and five of its member locals had refused to work on the Gateway Arch, a monument financed by the National Park Service, in order

---

——IS TO BUILDING TRADES
AS ——IS TO LILY WHITE

1) *Czolgosz is to Booth as McKinley is to a) Lincoln, b) Washington, c) Roosevelt, d) Garfield.*
2) *Aztec is to Mexico as Maya is to a) Peru, b) Guatemala, c) Haiti, d) Uruguay.*
3) *——— is to phlegmatic as vivacious is to ———.*
   1. husky 2. rheumatic 3. pneumatic 4. sluggish
   A. elusive B. pouting C. exuberant D. gripping
4) *——— is to composer as Longfellow is to ———.*
   1. Dali 2. Van Gogh 3. Riley 4. Haydn
   A. musician B. poet C. entertainer D. president
5) *Revolution is related to evolution as flying is to*
   1. birds 2. whirling 3. walking 4. wings 5. standing

Questions like these are likely to give even college graduates pause. Yet they parallel questions on tests that potential building-trades artisans are required to pass. Pressed hard to integrate by the federal government and civil-rights groups, a number of building-trades unions are now screening candidates for their apprenticeship programs with seemingly objective aptitude tests given by professional testing agencies. But the tests themselves are a subtle form of discrimination against young men from minority groups.

---

to block employment of non-A.F.L.-C.I.O plumbers. The contractor, the Hoel-Steffen Construction Co., had attempted to fulfill the nondiscrimination clause in its contract. Since the Plumbers' local did not have a single Negro among its 1,200 members and 102 apprentices, Hoel-Steffen was forced to look beyond the A.F.L.-C.I.O. hiring hall. It subcontracted the work to a firm with three Negro plumbers.

When the Negro plumbers reported to the job, the Building Trades Council announced that its members would cease work because the project was not completely staffed with A.F.L.-C.I.O. members. The union boycott brought work to a halt. The Justice Department then charged the council and four of its member unions with discriminating against Negroes. The National Labor Relations Board also found the unions guilty of an unfair labor practice.

An injunction forced the A.F.L.-C.I.O. unions to complete work on the Gateway Arch. And charges against the Plumbers and Pipefitters were dropped when they agreed to eliminate discriminatory practices. However, Justice's case against the electrical and sheet-metal unions was still pending two years later. There the government was seeking a verdict that would force the unions to accept Negro journeymen and apprentices whose qualifications are equal to those of the least-qualified white member initiated since 1961.

Boycotts by building-trades unions are commonplace, but union officials always insist that these work stoppages are not motivated by racial prejudice. However, shortly after the boycott of the Gateway Arch project, the St. Louis Trades Council again ordered its members to walk off a construction project rather than work with Negro electricians who by early 1968 were not members of the A.F.L.-C.I.O. union. (At the time, no Negro in St. Louis had an Electrical

Workers' card permitting him to work on a construction project; today, twelve do.) Ironically, the project was an FHA-financed housing development sponsored by two Negro churches.

In 1967, in another case attacking union hiring-hall practices, the N.A.A.C.P. filed suit on behalf of Negroes who had sought employment on a $12,800,000 construction job on the campus of Ohio State University. Without membership in A.F.L.-C.I.O. unions, the Negroes were turned down by four contractors, who normally hired through union referrals. The court ruled that by acquiescing to the discriminatory practices of the contractors and the unions the state violated the Fourteenth Amendment of the Constitution. In a landmark decision, Judge Joseph P. Kinneary of the Federal District Court ruled that the state must see that contractors do not discriminate and must ensure that they seek hiring sources other than union halls if necessary.

If the precedent in the Ohio case is followed in other courts, the N.A.A.C.P. could halt all public construction where Negroes are not granted equal access to employment. "On public-works projects, Negroes are entitled to an equal share of the jobs," says Roy Wilkins, executive director of the N.A.A.C.P. "Negroes have been receiving only the crumbs of expenditures for public construction. This inequity must be stopped even if it means an indefinite moratorium on all public construction."

Another important step was taken in February, 1968, when pressure applied by Secretary of Labor Willard Wirtz produced a pledge by the eighteen building trades unions to begin active recruiting of Negro youths as apprentices. While this was a major blow to discrimination, so few openings occur that no more than 5000 Negroes could hope to enter these unions the first year.

In contrast to the craft unions, industrial unions have never excluded Negroes from membership. But many have codified, by collective-bargaining contracts, seniority systems that prevent Negroes from moving into higher-paying jobs. Says a federal official, "In seniority cases, industrial unions are fighting just as hard as the building-trades unions are in excluding Negroes." Discriminatory seniority systems were devised at a time when both labor and management believed that it was an acceptable practice to define certain areas of employment as "white" or "Negro." A job as a crane operator in a steel plant, for example, or as a tool-and-die maker for an auto company, was automatically filled by a white man. Similarly, a job as a hogshead dumper in a tobacco plant was a "Negroes only" task. Because of this, Negro lines of promotion ended at the semiskilled level.

The industrial unions have made little or no attempt to change the seniority system since they organized the basic industries in the 1930's. Now, however, they are being forced under the law to eliminate discrimination. But if all qualified workers are included in seniority units, should Negroes be allowed to displace whites who have advanced because of unfair privileges in the past? Should employers be allowed to introduce testing procedures when they open up "white" jobs to bids from Negroes? Are unions guilty of unfair labor practices when they agree to departmental seniority, which divides a plant into exclusive seniority units, and thus prevents those in the lowest-paid jobs from advancing? The Justice Department, the N.A.A.C.P. Legal Defense Fund, and others have court cases pending that touch on these and other arcane areas of seniority and promotion. And just as in the case of the building-trades unions, the industrial unions are under pressure from their white members who are loath to see an end to a system that gives them not only higher social status and a better income, but more job security than Negroes. Many white workers fear that if Negro and white seniority systems are merged, Negroes with longer service on the job will bump whites downward on the seniority ladder and thus make them more vulnerable to layoffs. This combination of fear and bigotry is not to be underestimated, especially in the South. In 1967, when Armstrong Rubber promoted a Negro, Wharlest Jackson, in its Natchez, Mississippi, plant, Jackson was murdered.

Well aware of what they are up against, civil-rights groups attacking discriminatory seniority systems are going to considerable lengths to assuage union fears that changes in the system will immediately penalize their white members. The N.A.A.C.P. Legal Defense Fund, for example, has sued Philip Morris and Local 203 of the Tobacco Workers International Union on the grounds that a seniority system in the company's Richmond, Virginia, plant freezes Negroes into low-paying jobs. But the Fund, while asking that Negroes have an opportunity to progress upward in the plant, has asked the court not to penalize white workers whose job or seniority status could be construed as a result of past discrimination.

More complaints of restrictive seniority and promotion practices have been lodged against the United Steelworkers and the steel industry than any other group. Since July, 1965, no fewer than 321 complaints have been filed by the N.A.A.C.P. against steelworker locals and individual companies. (Most of the complaints involve southern mills.)

In January, 1968, three court actions were pending against the union and U.S. Steel. One of these cases grew out of a history of discrimination in the U.S. Steel, Fairfield, Alabama, plant. For many years, jobs in this plant were graded numerically from one to fourteen. Negroes could not advance beyond grade six, crane helpers, while whites could progress to the best-paid union job in the plant, locomotive cranemen. In 1963, the union and management agreed to merge the two lines and allow Negroes to move into higher-rated jobs after two years.

The following year, however, the union and the company abrogated the agreement. Instead, they set up three separate seniority rosters with the best-paying jobs in one group, the mid-range jobs in a second, and the menial jobs to which Negroes had been restricted in a third. Negroes could request a transfer from the third group to one of the other seniority groups whenever a vacancy occurred. However, their seniority would date from the time of entry into the new job group. For example, a Negro with years of experience as a crane helper would have to forfeit all his seniority in order to enter a line of progression that led to a job as a crane operator. Since employment in the steel industry is declining, and seasonal layoffs are common, seniority is a vitally important buffer against unemployment. Thus, the Negroes' inability to transfer to another line of progression while retaining seniority would make him more vulnerable to layoff.

Except for the Steelworkers, no industrial union has come under fiercer attack for discrimination than the International Ladies' Garment Workers', a New York-based union once considered the most militant fighter for social justice in the labor movement. Roy Innis, chairman of the Harlem chapter of the Congress of Racial Equality, charges that "I.L.G.W.U. has for years permitted conditions to exist which keep the vast majority of black workers in the lowest-paying jobs and has denied black workers a policy-making voice in the union through restrictive constitutional provisions." Similar charges have been made by the N.A.A.C.P. Herbert Hill claims that the union, which has about 150,000 non-white members out of a total of 450,000, has negotiated wages for jobs held mostly by non-whites that are only slightly above the minimum wage, while it has negotiated handsome pay raises for cutters and pressers who are mostly white.

Since 1963, the I.L.G.W.U., and its companion needletrades union, the Amalgamated Clothing Workers of America, have opposed federally sponsored training programs for the garment industry despite a shortage of skilled workers. The unions argued that training inexperienced workers is the employer's job. And they combined to block federal funds for training programs in Newark and New York. Ironically, hundreds of cutters have been recruited in Italy to fill vacancies in the industry.

At the same time, the I.L.G.W.U. effectively bars most members from running for election as president or secretary-treasurer of the union. To be eligible for these offices, a candidate must be a delegate to the convention, a member of the union for ten years, and a paid officer of the union for five years. Relatively few Negroes meet these requirements. And while they apply to all members, civil-rights leaders contend that such requirements effectively prohibit proportional representation for Negroes in the upper ranks of the union. No Negro has ever been elected to the general executive board of the union. (One Puerto Rican has.)

CORE has been trying to organize Negro members of the I.L.G.W.U. to press for constitutional reform and a new wage policy. But the response has been poor, in part because the union's constitution also prohibits the formation of caucuses, groups, and clubs within the union, except for a brief period prior to the convention. With bitter humor, Negroes call the I.L.G.W.U. "Dubinsky's plantation" (a reference to the peppery labor leader who helped found the union).

Although job discrimination is flatly outlawed by the Civil Rights Act, Negro leaders complain that so far it has been difficult to get the government to enforce the law effectively and quickly. Under Title VII of the act, a five-member Equal Employment Opportunity Commission is authorized to deal with job discrimination complaints. If the complaints are valid, the commission must attempt to get compliance by conciliation. If the unions fail to comply, the individual bringing the charges must allow state agencies sixty days to eliminate the discriminatory practice. If the state agencies fail, the commission can refer the matter to the Justice Department. Justice, however, will prosecute only if it believes that there is a broad pattern of discrimination. And, by the beginning of 1968, Justice had filed only five suits under Title VII of the Civil Rights Act against unions—four against the Electrical Workers and one against the Asbestos Workers.

The individual victim of discrimination can, of course, file his own suit against a union or employer. But without the financial and legal aid of civil-rights organizations, few Negroes can afford to embark on expensive litigation. Legislation now in Congress would enable the Equal Employment Opportunity Commission to issue cease-and-desist orders, a power similar to that held by the National Labor Relations Board.

One federal agency that has opened up employment areas hitherto closed to Negroes is the Office of Federal Contract Compliance. This agency has the power to insist on affirmative action against racial discrimination by companies bidding on government contracts over $50,000. A plea that a company cannot correct racial imbalance because it is forced to accept labor supplied by unions is no defense. "We don't accept that," says the OFCC's director, Edward C. Sylvester Jr. "We say, 'If you can't deliver equal opportunity, don't expect government contracts. It's your responsibility to bargain.'" By threatening to withhold a $120-million contract for four nuclear submarines, the government forced the Newport News Shipbuilding & Dry Dock Co. and several unions, including the Machinists, to change discriminatory job practices. A federal grant of $13 million to San Francisco's Bay Area Rapid Transit System was blocked until the government got a guarantee of affirmative action by the contractors and unions involved. And even the building-trades unions put 112 skilled Negroes to work when threatened with cancellation of federal construction contracts in Ohio.

Ever since the merger of the A.F.L. and C.I.O. in 1955, Negro leaders have tried, without success, to get help from white union leaders. In those cases where Negro members have sought legal aid to redress their grievances against locals, the A.F.L.-C.I.O. has never volunteered assistance, or entered a case as a friend of the court. Moreover, Negro leaders who have challenged the labor movement have been answered with personal abuse. Some years ago A. Philip Randolph, a vice president of the A.F.L.-C.I.O., asked the federation to expel unions that practice segregation. Randolph's dignity and integrity have made him a recognized spokesman for the Negro, but George Meany answered his plea with a roar of anger. Said Meany, "Who in the hell appointed you as guardian of the Negro members in America?"

Some Negro leaders now believe that the chasm between Negroes and labor unions is unbridgeable. As a result, both the N.A.A.C.P. and CORE are encouraging the formation of all-Negro unions outside the A.F.L.-C.I.O. Cleveland Robinson, international vice president of the Retail, Wholesale and Department Store Workers and national president of the Negro American Labor Council, explains, "The cry of the Negro is this: if labor will not open its doors, then we will have to form our own organizations." Negro craftsmen in Cleveland, Chicago, and Cincinnati have organized independent unions. And CORE has set up the Maryland Freedom Union to organize Negroes in retail trade and service industries.

A report issued by the Maryland group, which has negotiated contracts for hospital and retail store workers in Baltimore, illustrates the threat posed to the A.F.L.-C.I.O. by independent Negro unions. The report states: "The labor protest movements of the 1930's have become 'business unions,' large stable organizations removed from the masses of unskilled and semiskilled workers with earnings below the national poverty level for a family of four. The two million northern black people who work in retail and service trades remain almost as unorganized as they had been in 1935, when the Retail Clerks International Association began to increase its membership. The approximately 100,000 black union members in northern retail and service jobs represent a pitifully small percentage of those potentially organizable. In the Baltimore area alone, there are approximately 40,000 potentially organizable workers. The Maryland Freedom Union proposes to establish a structure through which thousands of unorganized, low income, unskilled workers can be reached."

Moderates, such as Bayard Rustin, head of the A. Philip Randolph Institute, still feel that Negroes must work within organized labor to end existing abuses. Among other things, Rustin argues that the mood of the country is such that a "black power" labor movement would be quickly crushed. However, if labor leaders continue to frustrate Negro demands for entry into the building-trades unions and equal treatment in the industrial unions, even moderate Negroes will have to reappraise their relationship with organized labor.

Considering the size and importance of the problem, there has been relatively little pressure on the labor movement to reform its racial policies. Politicians who depend on labor's votes to remain in office cannot afford to condemn the unions' racial policies. Nevertheless, if organized labor is to avoid a complete split with the civil-rights movement, it must eliminate restrictive practices. Four major reforms would help transform the labor movement from a privileged club into an open democratic institution:

¶ The union hiring hall must be eliminated. Unions still control an estimated two million jobs through such arrangements. Employers should be free to hire any qualified worker.

¶ Unions guilty of racial discrimination should be expelled by the A.F.L.-C.I.O. and decertified.

¶ The Labor Department should ensure free entry into apprenticeship programs and, in cooperation with state agencies, should ensure that sufficient manpower is recruited to eliminate the shortage of skilled craftsmen.

¶ Unions with constitutional provisions that prevent any member from campaigning or running for office should be decertified by the N.L.R.B. Although Negroes constitute about 13 percent of union membership, they have little representation on the policy-making bodies of unions.

All of these recommendations, of course, would change the character of the labor movement dramatically. But labor needs to be reformed. The last barriers to the caste system in American society are falling and labor, like other institutions, must be prepared to make sacrifices to allow the democratic ideal of equality to become a reality.

7

"OUR WAR
WAS WITH THE
POLICE DEPARTMENT"

by Eleanore Carruth

A lot of hope for the peaceful future of the city is invested in
"community relations" programs established by police departments throughout the country. One of the most highly
regarded of such programs has been that of the San Francisco
police department. Its Community Relations Unit has been
praised in a report prepared for the President's Crime Commission for opening "new communication channels with
community segments never before considered 'reachable.' "
It has been commended by San Francisco civic groups and
praised by Negroes themselves for "really doing something."
Yet the man who made this program a national example of
how to do it left in despair after five years on the job. His experience tells a lot about what it takes to make community-
relations programs work, and why most of them don't work
very well.

Dante Andreotti was a twenty-one-year veteran of the
San Francisco police force when, in 1962, Chief Thomas Cahill named him to head the department's newly created
Community Relations Unit. The original directive to the
unit (Andreotti plus an assistant at the outset) was to go
out into the community and teach respect for law and order.

"I was naive. I went out into the community and I got bruised. Community relations is not selling the police product. If the product were salable you wouldn't have to have community relations. . . . Explaining the police department is something you can do after you have proved yourself. You can communicate or fat-mouth to your heart's content, but if people don't see tangible results happening in other areas of their lives, you have lost them. The word gets around that you can't do anything."

Andreotti set about trying to do things. He held meetings, as he was supposed to, "and when you hold meetings, you get complaints." Andreotti and his men listened, wrote up the complaints, directed them to the police chief or to other city agencies, and frequently followed up on them. "I guess I rocked the boat, but sometimes you have to rock a few boats to get things done."

That beginning won a lot of support for Andreotti among minority groups, Mexicans and Chinese as well as Negroes. It also gave him insight into the needs of his constituency. "To be effective, we had to address ourselves to social problems that could lead to police problems. We had to be involved, get around, know what the order of the community was. We practically lived in the neighborhoods." Among other things, Andreotti and his men:

¶ Coached Negro boys for union examinations to help them qualify as apprentices.

¶ Raised money for a wide range of needs, from new plumbing for a recreation center to clothing for Negroes applying for jobs. Sometimes donations took the form of goods rather than money. Andreotti got Carpenters Union officials, for instance, to donate tools to an organization of Negro boys so they could learn some carpentry while fixing up their club

123

quarters in a warehouse. (He also got a local civil-rights group to pick up the club's utility bills.)

¶ Worked with Upward Bound, the federal program to get underprivileged youngsters thinking in terms of college. Upward Bound "enrolled" potential high-school dropouts in special six-week courses at the local state college and put them up in dormitories so they could get the feel of student life. To ease the tensions of an unfamiliar situation, Andreotti's men went to the campus, talked to the kids, even stayed overnight sometimes to give them a sense of security.

¶ Interpreted the police records of job applicants to prospective employers. Policemen went with applicants to job interviews and indicated where offenses were minor or there were extenuating circumstances. In a single six-month period one officer alone "explained" 200 Negroes into jobs.

"Only the people themselves," argues Andreotti, "can say whether a program is working." By that measure, his program appeared to be working. "We really related to them," says one San Francisco Negro.

But in the course of winning friends in the slums, Andreotti antagonized most of the police department. "The police in general," he says, "look upon community relations as something of minor importance. They regard it as something forced upon them by the Negroes, not as something they want to do out of their hearts. They want to be efficient. You can get technically efficient as hell, but if you are not effective with people you might as well close shop. Our war was with the police department. We were never successful in getting the message down to the foot soldier: that community relations is the most important job.

"I sincerely believe that policemen are hung up on this law-and-order bit. They forget the law part. Too many of them regard the law as something that they impose upon the people and not as something that protects people's rights. Too many policemen feel they have to show they are the boss on the street. Instead of trying to communicate with the Negro, to make him feel that the law is for him too, they are busy espousing the thin-blue-line theory, the idea that they stand between you and chaos. The system itself contributes to the cynicism, the feeling of isolation, that many policemen have."

Andreotti estimates that fully 90 percent of the San Francisco police force was hostile toward the community-relations program. As a lieutenant, he got no lip from the rank and file, but his staff had to put up with a lot of taunts from fellow policemen. How do you like working in the commie-relations department? Have they brainwashed you yet? Have you got your N.A.A.C.P. card? You're the biggest nigger-lover in the police department. "There was John Birch literature on the bulletin boards in some precincts," Andreotti recalls. "One of them had a large picture of the Imperial Wizard of the Ku Klux Klan with a headline reading 'Our Hero.' "

Andreotti's pleas for wider police participation in the program went unheeded. He once sent out a teletype to all precincts inviting the entire force to the annual Christmas party of the neighborhood Community Relations committees; not one man came. When he tried to recruit police basketball teams to compete against neighborhood teams, only one white policeman responded. A drive to find young Negroes to fill a number of low-grade jobs that were available ran into the same stony negativism. Andreotti met with the precinct captains and asked them to have their men, in the course of routine duties, find youngsters who wanted jobs, fill out a simple card form for each job seeker, and return it to the

Community Relations Unit. He didn't get a single return.

The role of Chief Cahill throughout was "ambiguous," according to Andreotti. "He supported us and yet he didn't support us." Cahill had difficulties of his own with the force's animosity toward community relations. A lot of grumbling from the ranks undoubtedly reached his ears.

In the beginning, says Andreotti, Cahill "went along with all the maverick ideas." He also gave Andreotti more staff— fifteen people, eventually. But Cahill refused Andreotti's request that he raise the general rank, and therefore the pay and status, of men detailed to the unit. And when Andreotti wanted to add more Negroes to the four he already had, "Cahill told me there were too many already. He said he thought one of them had been planted by the Muslims."

In September, 1966, a riot broke out after a police warning shot killed a Negro fleeing from a stolen car. Although the riot lasted five days and 160 people were injured, there were no additional deaths and very little property damage. The Community Relations Unit was generally credited with a major role in cooling the conflagration.

About a week after the riot, Andreotti relates, "Cahill said to me, 'I'll know how to handle this situation next time. After all I did for those people! I was the only police chief in America without a riot. They spoiled my record.' I told him, 'You ought to be damn glad you had a good community-relations program going.' "

Cahill beefed up special tactical units, trained in judo and karate, and sent them out in two-car, eight-man teams to handle potential "incidents." As time went by, Andreotti felt more and more that Cahill no longer supported his program, and that the new emphasis on force was impairing community relations. In August, 1967, Andreotti retired from the police department and went to work for the Community Relations Service of the U.S. Department of Justice. Police Chief Cahill was on vacation at the time and did not attend Andreotti's testimonial reception. Neither did the deputy chief nor any captain in the San Francisco police department.

Andreotti points out that the police are not entirely to blame for the ineffectiveness of community-relations programs. "To be truly successful, a community-relations program must get support from the very top and from the whole community." He didn't get that kind of support. George Christopher, mayor of the city in the early years of the program, "wasn't behind it," says Andreotti. "He never went to a community-relations meeting." If policemen refused to help, so did businessmen. Andreotti once sent a form letter to 4,500 members of a San Francisco merchants' association, asking for jobs for Negroes. "After three months, we didn't get one summer job or a job of any kind." A televised plea along the same lines brought in hate mail, but no offers of jobs.

"A lot of people," Andreotti says, "have helped create the present impasse in community relations. It's not just the fault of the police. Others bear a large responsibility—the people who contributed to the decay of the city, the businesses that moved away, the middle class in its flight to the suburbs. Many segments of the community are responsible because they haven't addressed themselves to social and economic problems that have developed into police problems. The police are stuck because they are shouldering the burden of the larger community."

8

SYSTEMS ENGINEERING INVADES THE CITY

by Lawrence Lessing

In cities all over the U.S., police captains, garbage collectors, prison wardens, health officers, highway administrators, welfare workers, and other toilers in the urban bureaucracy are getting the feeling that strange men are looking over their shoulders. The strangers speak an odd jargon, spend days digging into musty files, prowl the offices asking prying questions. Their behavior is mystifying, sometimes irritating, to tradition-bound bureaucrats. But they represent one of the best hopes that have so far turned up for bringing orderly solutions to the disorderly problems of the city.

The strange intruders are systems engineers, and they come out of the far different world of the aerospace-electronics industry. They are trying to apply the techniques developed in building missiles and spacecraft to the down-to-earth problems that grow out of the way people live together. This is not as wild a jump as may first appear. For systems engineering is not merely a technique for producing exotic hardware; more basically, it is a new way of approaching complex problems and organizing their solution. The systems engineer gives the city a new view of itself, in which Negro poverty and traffic congestion and other urban maladies are not isolated problems to be treated one by one but are seen to be bound up in the whole interwoven context of an environment steadily becoming more unmanageable and unlivable.

The application of this promising new approach is still in its very early stages, but already a great deal of activity is going on. A major landmark is the group of four systems studies commissioned by the State of California in 1965 in the areas of crime control, information processing, transportation, and waste disposal. These were the first broad-scale experiments of their kind in local government. Since then, more and more major cities and some states have contracted for systems studies in a great variety of problems. New York and Philadelphia are setting up small internal systems-analysis groups of their own, so they will have the expertise to evaluate the studies they contract for. And the federal Demonstration Cities and Metropolitan Development Act of 1966 provides for the maximum feasible use of the systems approach in designing projects for its model-cities program; sixty-three such projects are scheduled to start in 1968.

Systems engineering presents business with a portentous opportunity for bringing its talents and resources to bear on urban problems. Not suprisingly, the pioneers in urban systems studies are the top aerospace-computer-electronics companies—such as Aerojet-General, Litton, Lockheed, G.E., North American Aviation, TRW, and I.B.M. Also moving into the field from once purely military systems analysis are such specialists as the Rand Corp., System Development Corp., and Planning Research Corp., the biggest profit-oriented firm in the systems-management consultant business. Late in 1967 retired Air Force General Bernard A. Schriever, who mobilized systems management for the development of the U.S. missile program, began organizing a consortium of ten or more leading aerospace, electronics, construction, and architectural-engineering companies to mount a concerted, broad-scale attack on the problem of making cities more workable.

To be sure, the programs under consideration have not yet got much beyond the study stage. Some people still have reservations as to how well the systems approach, previously oriented largely toward tangible hardware, can deal with the intangibles of society. Certainly, it is not, as one critique has put it, a "quick technological fix" for all urban ills. But the studies have gone far enough to show that systems techniques can be shaped into a powerful new planning tool for getting at the most obdurate problems, many of them, such as housing and transportation, inseparably physical and social in nature.

"Until we see the problem in its totality and understand its many ramifications," said Arjay Miller, then president of Ford Motor Co., which was the first to use systems techniques in the automobile industry and is now itself moving into the urban problem area, "we cannot expect more than piecemeal efforts and piecemeal results . . . We now have the power, if we can but learn to use it, to break the mold of social apathy, of resignation to age-old human ills, of continued tolerance of the wide cleavage between our aspirations and reality."

Historically, cities have grown by random accretion, the result of hundreds of thousands of individual decisions by private builders and public agencies, largely unrelated to one another except by accident. As populations grew to megalopolitan proportions, and technologies such as that of the automobile and the high-voltage power line exploded outward in all directions, this vigorous laissez-faire pattern began seriously to break down.

Nearly all the measures so far taken to repair the pattern,

from traditional city planning to urban renewal, have tended to follow on a somewhat bigger scale the same random, uncoordinated, piecemeal approach that generated the problems in the first place. Highways have been pushed through without regard for the human and residential blight they create, without any effort to balance them with other forms of transportation—and in the end without relieving congestion. Slums have been razed, only to erect in their stead more highways, or office buildings, or luxury apartments—while the displaced slum dwellers move off to decaying housing elsewhere. As problems mount in complexity, patchwork solutions tend to cancel one another out. A classic example is a 1967 New York City ordinance that called for an upgrading of apartment-house incinerators and closing down of substandard ones so as to reduce air pollution. If the ordinance had been enforced (which it couldn't be), it would simply have dumped an overwhelming burden of extra garbage on an already overburdened sanitation department.

Systems engineering would take a different tack. At its most ambitious, it would examine the city in the round as a total systems complex, interrelating all its demographic, economic, social, and physical components, with a view to arriving at more integrated solutions to the multiple problems. No one has yet analyzed a city in this way—or, as a systems engineer puts it, no one has designed a "systems model" of a city—for it is the most formidably complex of all systems dealt with so far. Ideally, the engineers would like to build a new city from the ground up, and some are working in this direction, in order to learn how to build old cities anew. On a more immediately practical plane, systems engineering offers a new way to look at individual large urban problems from all sides, weigh all possible alternative solutions with their costs and predictable consequences, and then get on with an optimum solution by the shortest possible route.

At the simplest level, systems engineering is just logical common-sense planning, not remarkably different from the procedure followed in other disciplinary pursuits. At its most sophisticated, it is an uncommon, intricately organized method for bringing to bear all relevant scientific, technical, and other resources upon the analysis and systematic solution of complex problems. In the process, it employs such mathematical tools as input-output techniques, linear and nonlinear programming, cost-effectiveness formulas, simulation modeling, feedback theory, queueing theory, and other esoteric techniques transposed from the physical sciences.

The orgins of the systems approach lie in the electrical industry and its manner of putting together great power and telephone and other communication systems. The Bell Telephone Laboratories was the earliest center and still remains the high seat of systems engineering. In World War II, with the infusion of a parallel development called operations research, systems techniques were used to accelerate the completion of such complex jobs as the development of radar and the atom bomb. Afterward these techniques began to reach maturity in such projects as the nuclear submarine, missiles and, at a new peak of complexity, sending men to the moon.

The systems approach was also enlisted in two notable civilian programs. The first, begun in 1956, was the Delaware River Basin project, an ambitious, coordinated attempt to improve the water and community resources of an entire river valley. The second was the Northeast Corridor Project to develop new high-speed train services between Boston and Washington, which is scheduled to enter a preliminary demonstration phase in the spring of 1968.

If there is a single instrument that brought systems techniques to ever wider application, it is the computer, which made possible the rapid storage and manipulation of vast amounts of data. Today the systems approach, in whole or part, has penetrated many government agencies, particularly the Department of Defense, and permeates most advanced industries, where it is effecting a new managerial revolution.

Wherever and however it is used, the systems approach follows roughly the same, very precise procedure. A program is generally composed, depending on the nature of the problem, of four or five distinct phases. The first two are called the systems-study (or program-planning) phase and the exploratory (or project-planning) phase; they are sometimes considered as one, for both are occupied with basic planning. In these phases the problem is defined or "structured," and the boundaries of the system are drawn—a city "system" might take in relationships all over its region. Next, all relevant data on the system and its environment are assembled, the field is searched for all feasible options for solving the problems, and the whole body of information is analyzed so as to narrow the choice down to the best solutions.

Once a managerial decision is made to proceed on the basis of this broad analysis, a third phase—known as the project, or development-planning, phase—begins. Now the solutions that seem best are studied in more detail; some are weeded out, others are put into research, and a projection is made of their development costs and the time they will take. The final managerial decision is then up to the agency that employs the systems engineers.

There are still two more phases, called "action" phases. First, the solution that has been selected is developed and tested through a prototype or pilot-project stage. And finally, after the system is installed, its total operations are monitored to ascertain whether it can be modified and its performance improved. On big projects the whole process has generally covered about a ten-year span, with planning closely coupled to action all along the way.

More important than the tools or procedures of the systems approach is the philosophy underlying its practice. The early planning usually involves a wide range of experts. The team examining the problem may include economists and ecologists as well as mathematicians, meteorologists, physicists, political scientists, and sociologists, with the systems engineers acting as idea brokers. A second feature of systems work is the translation of data, ideas, and observations into mathematical models. These can be fed into a computer, which simulates the system's operation and which can then be used to test the costs, effects, and operations of alternative solutions. In drawing up their array of possible solutions, the systems teams include not only well-tried devices and techniques, but also all the most advanced ideas and new technologies within reach, so that the system finally selected will not turn out to be obsolete by the time it is completed.

When a system gets the go-ahead, tight schedules are set up to meet a target date. This involves critical-path analysis —designating the sequence of critical components or new technology—and the parallel development of all components and subsystems, so that the whole complex comes together in working order by its due date. It is these techniques that have brought off such phenomenal feats as the first, flawless flight of the Apollo-Saturn V rocket on November 9, 1967.

The systems engineers who orchestrate this whole process are a new breed in very short supply. The first graduate program in systems engineering was begun in 1953 at the

University of Pennsylvania's Moore School of Electrical Engineering, birthplace of the first electronic computer. Similar programs have been started by leading engineering schools such as M.I.T., Stanford, and Johns Hopkins, but so far their output has been unable to keep up with demand.

The traditional figure of an engineer who prefers detailed work or specialization does not make a good systems man. He has to be interested in tackling broad problems from unorthodox angles. He is broad but not shallow, trained to some depth in a specialty—electrical engineering, mathematics, or whatever—but able to cross boundary lines into other disciplines and talk knowledgeably with specialists. This universalistic quality of the systems men is the major reason for hoping that their techniques can be fruitfully transferred to cities, where a major part of the challenge is to order and control sometimes conflicting solutions.

A major obstacle to this transfer of technique is the chaotic state of information gathering and data availability in cities. This is made worse by the fact that the managers of local governments are generally so unsophisticated that they are unable to deal adequately with the mountains of data they do accumulate. Some cities are trying to remedy the situation. New York, for example, has an arrangement with Rand Corp. to study how to apply the systems approach to budgeting, planning, and long-range policy development.

Perhaps the most comprehensive and instructive approach to the information problem has been Lockheed's study for the state of California. Its objective was to design a computerized information-handling system that would much more effectively take care of the present flow of information to and from the state's agencies, local government units, and the public, and provide for growth in the future.

135

First, the Lockheed systems engineers had to analyze th
total flow of information in the present system. In over 600 in
terviews with state and local officials, the team studied th
handling of such items as auto licenses, crime reports, jo
placements, tax returns, and other vital statistics. It foun
the volume of information growing at such a rate that b
1980 it would fill a string of filing cabinets stretching from Sac
ramento to Los Angeles. From this study the team constructe
a matrix chart showing that the information flow formed
mosaic of over 1,000 junction points or interfaces, which de
tailed the complexity of the system. About 40 percent of th
state's departments and all its larger counties were alread
using computers, but in such an isolated, unconnected wa
that most information exchange was still accomplished b
shuffling papers. Unless drastic improvements were made
the cost of information handling for the state governmen
alone could be expected to rise by 1980 to nearly $2 billion
year, mainly to pay for additional civil-service employees.

The Lockheed group examined five possible alternative so
lutions to the problem. The most extreme was a completel
centralized giant computer complex for the whole state
Analysis showed that this would be a costly, overcentralize
monstrosity. The solution that most nearly met the objective
was a federated system in which state and local agencie
would continue to operate their own computer installation
as before, but these would be linked into a computerized "in
formation central." This new agency would have two func
tional parts: a data network, which would act as a switchin
center to allow all computers in the system to communicat
with one another, and an information index, which woul
tell an inquiring agency where specific information could b
found in the system. Information could then be read out di

rectly from computer storage in a matter of minutes. This system, estimated to cost nearly $100 million over ten years of development, could eventually save the state an estimated $116 million a year, mainly in the elimination of paper work, duplicate records, and additional personnel.

Beyond the cost savings, the swift availability of comprehensive data would help agencies to deal more effectively with such other problems as crime and delinquency, health and welfare, education and employment, the areas where solid facts are not easily come by. Information on job openings, for example, could be compiled faster, and the openings could be more quickly matched to job needs in problem areas. Moreover, the swift compilation of other data never before available on an up-to-date basis—such as land-use statistics, economic and traffic trends—could provide some of the prerequisites for sound urban planning and systems design. Thus information technology may have much to contribute to the solution of many social problems.

One such social problem—crime and delinquency—was met head on in another of the California systems studies, undertaken by Space-General Corp., a subsidiary of Aerojet-General Corp. A systems-engineering group under John Kuhn, head of Space-General's systems studies, plunged into an investigation of the state's total system of justice, from police precincts through the courts, penal institutions, and parole boards to rehabilitation. It soon became apparent that the only person in a position to know all the ins and outs of the system as a whole was the offender, for various divisions of the system rarely communicated with one another. As a result, there was hardly any coordination in gathering data or setting objectives.

By using mathematical modeling, matrix techniques, and

other devices of systems engineering, Kuhn's group organized the chaotic data into a comprehensible picture of California's crime problem. It also came up with some useful insights: for example, that the sharp rise in crime was attributable not to any sudden breakdown in public morality or failure in law enforcement, but to the enormous increase in the number of fourteen-to-twenty-nine-year-olds, the age group that typically has the greatest concentration of lawbreakers.

A special study of Los Angeles County sought to determine whether certain population factors have tended to make some sectors of a city more trouble-prone than others. The highest concentration of unfavorable factors was found to be in Watts, which erupted in violence soon after the study was completed. This confirmation of their analysis encouraged the systems engineers to conclude that the collection of more refined population data would enable local authorities to take preventive measures and make police surveillance more effective.

The Space-General team also computed what it cost the state to apprehend, try, and punish various kinds of offenders over their lifetime. The figure turned out to average $5,800 for homicides, $16,900 for check forgers, because the forger is a repeater, whereas the murderer once paroled or released rarely kills again. From this it could be deduced that the state was spending a disproportionate amount of money on "nuisance" crimes. Furthermore, the cost could be reduced in some cases by the wise use of technology. For instance, the $55-million annual bill for check forgery could be cut significantly if a really forgery-proof check system could be developed.

The crime study was so provocative that Space-General got a contract to do a second study—on California's welfare system. The seemingly uncontrollable escalation of welfare costs is, of course, a major problem in many states, but California is tormented more than most. Its welfare budget is now running well over $1 billion a year. The Kuhn group found that the money was being poured out without any clearly defined objective. American society has never decided whether indigents are to be punished—some California officials, for example, have suggested that people on welfare should be put to forced labor in the fields of the San Fernando Valley—or whether the aim is to rehabilitate them into self-reliant workers. California's present system, in which welfare payments just cover bare subsistence, neither punishes nor rehabilitates, and there is widespread disenchantment over its dead-end effects.

The Space-General report, not yet released by the state, is only a feasibility study that arrives at no pat conclusions. It leaves open the question whether welfare recipients can be generally lifted to employable status; the available evidence is conflicting. The idea of combining training programs with economic subsidies such as the negative income tax is a widely discussed alternative to welfare, but it needs more study. But the Kuhn group did shatter some myths—for example, that welfare families beget welfare families. There is no substantive data to support that proposition. Indeed, the investigators found that welfare administrators do not even ask the simple question: have the recipient's parents ever been on relief? A continuing, organized, rational study is needed to get at the facts and find workable programs.

Systems engineers can more readily get their teeth into transportation, and that problem has probably had the greatest attention of any so far in systems studies. North American Aviation (now North American Rockwell) carried out the transportation study in the California series and produced a sweeping document that places the state's transportation needs for the rest of the century in context with a mathematical model of the total state economy, pinpointing the further detailed studies and programs needed.

The study that puts the urban traffic problem in sharpest focus is one being done for San Diego County. Called TRIP (meaning Transportation Requirements and Implementation Program), it was set up late in 1966 by a group of city and county governments acting in cooperation with their central planning agency. Ford Motor Co. and its subsidiary, Philco-Ford, are supplying the systems approach. The objective is to draw up the most comprehensive plan ever made, to guide the evolutionary development of all forms of transportation for a single urban region. A phase-one feasibility study has already been substantially completed. TRIP is now in the process of refining and testing its mathematical models of the San Diego region. These will project transportation demand in relation to urban growth, development, and demography, and provide the framework for testing by simulation the effects of various transportation schemes and new technologies.

Ford hopes to make San Diego a laboratory for the study of the transportation problems of all metropolises. That city has not yet reached the sprawling, smog-bound, traffic-snarled crisis stage of nearby Los Angeles, but it is on its way there. Like other West Coast cities, it is almost entirely dependent on the private automobile, with little public transport to speak of. Highways cannot be built fast enough to meet demand, and it is becoming clear that the mere building of more highways will not alone reduce congestion. At the same time, many people—especially the growing group of the retired—are without adequate means of transportation. A long-range systems program would bring some balance into the picture. Methods are becoming available for taking social and land-use factors into account in designing highways, and not simply depending on the highway engineer's formula for finding the shortest distance between two points at lowest cost. Systems are also emerging for a new type of drive-it-yourself public transport, using small in-town vehicles, semi- or all-electric, which would run at low cost and cause a minimum of air pollution.

All the problems so far dealt with in systems studies really relate to subsystems of the much larger over-all system—the city as a whole. It may be some time before a systems team takes on a whole city in all its aspects, but a small start in that direction may be made by the Department of Housing and Urban Development's new model-city program. "Model city" is a misnomer; the program actually involves selected neighborhoods or sections of cities.

Many systems men, however, believe that systems engineering can show what it really can do for urban problems only when it takes on the building of entirely new cities, completely outside the old ones. A number of so-called "new towns" have risen recently, such as Reston, Virginia, and Irvine, California, but nearly all of them have been relatively limited suburban developments, built without benefit of systems engineering, and they are not working out too well.

The nearest thing to a systems approach to a new city is Columbia, Maryland, which is beginning to rise on 14,000 acres of rolling country about midway between Baltimore and Washington. Conceived by James W. Rouse, an energetic Baltimore mortgage banker and developer of apartments and shopping centers, it is intended to have a population of 110,000 by 1980. To start with, a hypothetical economic model was set up, detailing all the land, structures, and utilities needed for a complete city of that size, and projecting its cost and the businesses and industries needed to sustain it. Then, with $50 million in long-term financing from Connecticut General Life Insurance, Teachers Insurance & Annuity, and the Chase Manhattan Bank, land was acquired, the economic model revised to fit it, the zoning accommodations negotiated, and development started. But not before a kind of *ad hoc* systems-type task force of sociologists, psychologists, medical men, and religious leaders was convened to work out with architects and planners all the social and institutional needs of the projected community.

The plan that developed, with constant testing through the economic model, comprised nine village or neighborhood-type communities and a downtown business center; a third of the land area was left for interweaving natural woodlands, parks, paths, and artificial lakes. Since the spring of 1967, close to 500 homes, garden apartments, and town houses have risen in the first of the villages, along with a bank, stores, and supermarket, and the population in January, 1968 stood at about 1,000. Three companies have already built plants that will employ some 2,500 workers. A wide range of incomes will be accommodated, with homes ranging from $13,000 to $15,000 and upward and rentals from $100. The economic model is revised quarterly to keep it responsive to the market and to control finances and the pace of development, which proceeds steadily on critical-path scheduling to keep the multitude of parallel projects going on simultaneously in phase to meet the end objectives.

Architectural critics have pronounced Columbia's design undistinguished—home construction is turned over to selected custom builders. But Rouse is mainly interested in solving some of the basic economics of new-town building, on which many architecturally distinguished plans have come a cropper.

From a systems-engineering standpoint, Columbia's largest deficiency is that it does not draw in or encourage technological innovation—all the potential new materials, building techniques, and systems that have gone unused in older, code-restricted city redevelopments, which might dramatically reduce costs.

Even Columbia represents a relatively limited-scale application of the systems approach. Systems engineering will not prove its true value unless it is used on a large scale. The first four California State projects were all only six-month, $100,000 study contracts, too brief and underfinanced to do more than indicate how aerospace techniques might be applied to the urban scene. Only one—Aerojet-General's waste-disposal study—has survived California's change of state administration; it has gone into a phase-two development program for Fresno County. San Diego's TRIP is waiting for funds so it can get on to the next planning phase. And HUD's model-city program, which got only half of its current year's budget request, or $300 million, is forced to spread its funds so thin that most of them will go to fighting immediate fires rather than to comprehensive systems programs to eliminate the causes of fire.

To get beyond the study phase, urban-systems programs need a long-term, heavy commitment of funds. The Vietnam war appears to stand in the way of such a commitment now. But even aside from that, the broad systems approach to urban problems must contend with politicians' lack of comprehension, the shifts and vagaries of administration, national apathy and antipathy toward long-range planning, the jealousies of professional and special interests, and the incredible fragmentation of federal, state, and local governments. In the federal sphere alone, more than ten departments or agen-

cies handle aspects of the big-city problem. No single agency
—or single purpose—guides the urban program, as NASA
does in space or the Pentagon in weaponry. The major problem therefore is to find some profit-oriented mechanism by
which the great talents of systems-oriented industry can be
brought to bear on the great needs of cities.

It is to this problem of finding a workable mechanism that
the as yet unnamed Schriever consortium of systems-oriented
companies is addressing itself. General Schriever, who retired
from the Air Force in 1966 to set up a management-con-
sultant firm, Schriever Associates, is convinced that systems
management can go far to help solve the large problems growing apace in the megalopolitan area. "The systems-analysis
approach," he says, "is the only way you can come up with
master planning." He had watched the fumbling attempt of
aerospace companies to do something in this unfamiliar, frac-
tionated area, not merely from a desire to diversify their
business but from a feeling that they owed it to the country
to participate in solving the problems. Schriever concluded
that what was needed was a consortium of about ten companies of sufficient breadth, stature, and diversified experience
to take on the big problems. Each would put in a modest
amount of money to spread costs and risks, each would contribute talent to the staff, yet none would have more than a
stock interest in the enterprise, thus preserving the consortium's balance and objectivity. By late 1967, he had put
together a core of members: Aerojet-General, American Ce-
ment, Control Data, Emerson Electric, Lockheed, Northrop,
Ralph M. Parsons (architectural engineering), and Raytheon.

The consortium would do the over-all studies, research,
and systems analysis of urban problems on a collective basis,
drawing on the best resources of its member companies, and

pulling in experts from such disciplines as sociology, the kind of men hardware companies do not normally employ. Projects would be put out for competitive bids, as is the practice with NASA and the Defense Department, and member companies would be given no preference in the bidding.

The consortium would not only offer federal, state, and local governments a capability to study their problems, but it would also manage the execution of their programs on a contract basis, supervising their completion down to the last rivet. The way things work now, systems hardware companies cannot properly act as prime contractors and managers of total programs, while systems consultant specialists do not have the means of executing programs. The consortium would bridge that gap, and it looks like a fruitful way to harness the profit motive to social ends. "This job," says General Schriever, "needs to be done at the supersystem level, dealing with *total* city systems."

What is needed, as systems men such as Litton's John H. Rubel have suggested, is a single big-city or new-town demonstration of the best that late twentieth-century thinking and technology can do to make a more workable urban environment. Such a huge demonstration program would cost a great deal, and might take ten to fifteen years to show substantial results. But if billions can be committed to a supersonic aircraft program, designed to reduce travel times for that fraction of the population that can afford it, why then cannot billions be committed to a demonstration for the benefit of a whole people that city life can be made more worth living? Such a demonstration project would spin off innumerable immediate side benefits, ideas, and transferable developments—not the least of which would be the promise that great city problems can indeed be solved.

9

MORTGAGES
FOR
THE SLUMS

by Walter McQuade

In September, 1967, a group of seven businessmen called on President Johnson with an extraordinary proposal. They would divert $1 billion of their investment funds from normal channels and apply them instead to the cause of upgrading real estate in urban slums. The businessmen were leaders of the American life-insurance industry; they represented three trade associations with 348 member companies that have combined assets of $159 billion and invest some $17 billion yearly—scarcely any of it, up to now, in the slums.

At the meeting the President glowed and his Secretary of Housing and Urban Development, Robert C. Weaver, a less demonstrative man, looked deeply pleased. The insurance men themselves, whose main spokesman during the proceedings was Gilbert Fitzhugh, chairman of the Metropolitan Life Insurance Co., looked happy too. After the meeting, presidential aide Joseph Califano ushered them into the Fish Room with Secretary Weaver to face the press—and at this point things became a bit less sugary. At the end of thirty-five minutes of questioning, it must have been clear to all concerned that explaining to the public just what they were up to wouldn't be easy. Some of the reporters registered skepticism that the industry would accomplish much, and most of them seemed a little confused about the mechanics of the proposal. At one point, a reporter asked: "What will be the criteria you use to give away this money?" Fitzhugh replied tartly, "We are not giving away anything."

Fitzhugh is a man who is ordinarily open and candid. But in this case, possibly in an effort to avoid seeming sanctimonious, he may have been ducking the issue. The contribution by the life-insurance companies to the well-being of U.S. urban society will be considerable. It is true that the contributions will not take the form of outright gifts; the billion dollars will be *invested* in the slums, and the investment will, in general, be profitable. But it will be far less profitable than alternative investments. The difference in the returns may very plausibly be considered as a self-imposed "tax," designed to speed social progress—and it may be a big tax. Consider, for example, the companies' first investments under the program. Within a month of the announcement, they had committed $27,500,000 in mortgages on slum dwellings, investments that will yield just about 6 percent interest—in a mortgage market where they could easily have achieved returns ranging from 6.75 to 7.5 percent.

Despite the catcalls of skeptics, this move by one of the most conservative of large American industries is built on some quite statesmanlike notions. To see why statesmanship is required, it will pay to start with the fact that the slums have had a distinctly negative appeal for investment money.

The main difficulty with real-estate investment in the slums is that the investments are risky and, accordingly, attract only high-return capital—and very little of that. "In some of these blighted areas," Fitzhugh observed recently, "the interest rate on mortgages may be 25 percent. And even if you can pay that, just try and get a mortgage in Harlem." In recent years, and especially after 1967's riots, the private investment pattern in the slums has generally been one of *dis*-investment.

To get money flowing back into the slums, the government has been trying to create several investment channels. There is one very clear channel, dug in 1965, through which is now flowing most of the insurance money so far committed. The channel was opened when Congress passed what came to be known as the Rent Supplement Act. The act is perhaps best known for a provision that enables low-income families to obtain decent housing by helping them pay the rent with federal subsidies. They pay 25 percent of their income in rent; government contributes the rest. But because the supply of adequate low-cost housing is so short, it is also necessary to encourage the building of more, and the Federal Housing Administration is the instrument chosen to do that. FHA stimulates private investment by insuring mortgages covering up to 100 percent of total costs. Interest on the mortgages being insured is not allowed to exceed 6 percent.

The introduction of the rent-supplement program drew applause from almost all political audiences. It was aimed directly at the low-income groups, and yet could be applied so that families of various income levels would become neighbors, thereby avoiding the deadly concentration of lower social groups that has marked most public housing. It also appeared that private mortgage money would be available because Congress was committed to paying a substantial part of the rent until the tenants came up in the world and could pay it all themselves.

But the act, passed in August, 1965, was in trouble by the time the program went into operation late in 1966. The problem was that the 6 percent mortgage return, which had seemed attractive when Congress acted, became unattractive because money rates rose sharply. It soon became obvious that the Federal National Mortgage Association, familiarly known as Fanny Mae, was the only likely taker of the rent-supplement mortgages. Fanny Mae would finance them under its "special assistance" program, which offers mortgages for projects deemed to be socially urgent that are unattractive to private investors. But it was also obvious that Fanny Mae would be stretching its emergency fund uncomfortably when it tried to cover all the rent-supplement construction. Building might have been quite constricted as a result.

The insurance companies' commitment undid this predicament. The companies have already virtually supplanted Fanny Mae as buyers of rent-supplement mortgages, and there is no longer any question about the availability of mortgage money. There is, however, a question about Congress' willingness to vote funds for the supplemental rent; and this may prove to be the limiting consideration in estimating how much the insurance companies might ultimately put into the rent-supplement mortgages. Right now $200 million to $300 million is considered the probable range of commitment. If there were no limits at all, and the companies decided to put the entire $1 billion into rent-supplement mortgages, they could finance 80,000 housing units.

A second channel, through which a substantial part of the $1 billion will probably flow, is Section 203 (b) of the National Housing Act, which enables FHA to insure mortgages on one- to four-family houses. The program has served in the past as the federal government's main instrument for encouraging private home ownership. Until quite recently, virtually all of this encouragement has taken place in the suburbs. FHA did not write much 203 (b) insurance in the depressed areas of the cities because Congress had directed it to insure mortgages only in "stable" neighborhoods—which most slum neighborhoods are not. But the agency came under congressional attack for its single-minded support of the suburbs. A year ago FHA was ordered to give slum mortgages more consideration despite the higher risks. It took local FHA offices a long time to get going. But by late November, 1967, 203 (b) loans were being processed at a rate of 500 a week. Most of these were very small—the 500 aggregated only about $5 million—and any such rate, if sustained, would imply an investment potential of some $250 million a year for the insurance men.

Investments under 203 (b) will be no sure thing for the insurance companies. At the press conference in Washington, Fitzhugh was asked whether the companies could still lose money on mortgages insured by the government. He answered, "Yes, we sure can. We hope not much." He was referring to the fact that the companies' loans under this law would be small ones and would typically involve high servicing charges. On the other hand, they will presumably have a high "social payoff." The thought has often been expressed that home ownership in the slums would restrain riots there.

Not all of the $1 billion will go to insured housing. Some of it, possibly a lot, will be invested in slum housing where neither the Rent Supplement Act nor Section 203 (b) are used, but where the companies see opportunities to invest profitably, although more dangerously than usual, in uninsured housing at market rates—i.e., at the rates prevailing in more stable areas. In effect, then, the companies will be investing in residential mortgages in two different ways: some money will be invested at less than market rates, with government insurance; some will be invested at market rates, but in high-risk markets where mortgage money has generally been unavailable.

Finally, some of the $1 billion will probably go into mortgages on commercial or industrial buildings in slums, to support companies that look like good risks and might create a significant number of jobs. By present standards, most companies in the slums are not good risks. One way to diminish the risk is being demonstrated in a new program conceived by the Small Business Administration. The program guarantees businessmen's lease rental payments in urban areas for as long as twenty years. The insurance companies have been eyeing this program with great interest.

Meanwhile, their funds will not be languishing. There is no doubt that they will be able to commit the entire $1 billion within two years. The companies plan to keep track of the investments carefully, to report regularly on their progress, and to make sure that no conventional investments are counted as part of the program. The companies are, in fact, already hinting quietly at another billion behind the first one, and their action is evidently stirring other financing giants. Robert Wood, assistant secretary of H.U.D., recalled in December, 1967, "I've been in this job for twenty-two months. For the first six months I had an aerospace syndrome: the people who wanted to solve our housing problems seemed to come mostly from high-technology companies that wanted to use their 'systems' capabilities. But now we have something more immediately practical: companies and associations coming in here with very high-caliber financing at the ready."

In one respect, the insurance companies have been remarkably lucky in the timing of their $1-billion venture. Since the program was first conceived, interest rates have turned up sharply. Now that it is time to invest the money, the companies can do so at extraordinarily high levels: 6 percent is "below the market" nowadays, but it is still higher than the rates on most of the mortgages in the companies' portfolios —and, many investors believe, higher than the rates that will prevail in the market a couple of years from now.

At the same time, high mortgage rates are making the companies' investments more valuable. Low-income housing is even more tightly pinched for capital in the present money market than other kinds of building. The $1-billion investment is a kind of demonstration that the private sector can work effectively in support of government-created social programs—and can generate some significant programs of its own.

10

WHAT BUSINESS CAN DO FOR THE CITIES

by the Editors of FORTUNE

The crisis in race relations, as this book shows, is of manageable proportions. The gloom that enshrouded our cities after the 1967 riots was based partly on an overstatement of the problem and partly on an underestimate of the resources we could bring to bear on it. Two chapters, one on the objective condition of American Negroes, the other on their subjective attitudes, suggest that things just were not as bad as they seemed. Negroes' incomes, jobs, housing, and education have been getting significantly better in recent years—and Negroes, in general, know it. They have a strong sense that they are more respected—i.e., by whites—than they were a few years ago. And what they want most of all for the future is not more violence and rioting, but more education for their children, more good jobs for themselves, and less segregation. On the whole, they seem to be eminently sensible both in their appraisals of the recent past and in their hopes about the immediate future.

Fire-eaters like Stokely Carmichael and Rap Brown may be able to scare the daylights out of white Americans who catch their acts on television, but they command far less respect in the Negro community than Martin Luther King or the National Association for the Advancement of Colored People. Which is not to say that most Negroes don't feel sorely aggrieved about some aspects of their lives; most of them do, and a rather sizable minority feel that, while the riots were bad, they served a useful purpose in prodding white America into action. White America, including the business community, cannot in general be proud of the sequence of events: much of the action that now seems most promising *was* triggered by the riots.

As for the action itself, businessmen must feel a mixture of pride and puzzlement about the rather special resources they have been marshaling in this crisis. If we were obliged to rely nowadays on the agencies that have traditionally dealt with urban Negroes' problems, we should indeed be in despair: who could still be hopeful that city hall, the welfare department, the local Democratic organization, the labor unions, the churches, and the schools could somehow combine to do what must be done? Most of these have simply seemed overmatched by the problems involved; for many Americans, perhaps the single most dispiriting thought about 1967's riots was that one of the worst took place in Detroit—whose city administration had done as much as any in the U.S. to establish good "community relations" programs. The unions, some of which once did a lot to help unskilled workers upgrade themselves, and which used to work hard and seriously at civil rights, have done little for Negroes in recent years and are often formidable barriers to their advancement.

Implicit in the governmental appeals for help at all levels is an acknowledgment that large corporations are the major repository of some rather special capabilities that are now required. Business executives are increasingly identified as the most likely organizers of community-action programs, like the Urban Coalition and its local counterparts. Corporate managers often have the special close-quarters knowledge that enables them to visualize opportunities for getting at particular urban problems—e.g., the insurance companies' plans for investments in the slums. Finally, the new "systems engineering" capability of many corporations has opened up some large possibilities for dealing with just about any complex social problems.

The emergence of the systems engineers in the past decade has been accompanied by a profound change in the way we think about social problems. These should no longer be viewed as calling only for "experts" in particular fields, because very few social troubles, and certainly not those of the cities, can be neatly walled off in any one field—race relations, say, or slum clearance. The new wisdom about the cities begins with an awareness that race and housing and jobs and education and welfare all interact. Coping effectively with any one of these generally requires coping with several others at the same time. In place of experts, then, we need the kind of systematic thinking that is accustomed to tackling problems with many variables.

The notion that the urban situation might be dealt with in this manner by privately based organizations was pioneered by aerospace companies in California, and was for some time regarded elsewhere as an eccentric boondoggle. But the demand for these organizations' services in the cities has become intense enough to stimulate the organization of a consortium of about ten major aerospace, electronics, construction, and other companies that can afford a far-flung range of services to the cities. Washington has intimated that a new Office of Industry Participation might be developed there to work in conjunction with the Department of Housing and Urban Development. One of the functions of such an office would be to encourage corporations to get deeply into some of those intertwined urban problems, ordinarily on a contract basis. A single contract might, for example, involve designing as well as building houses for slum dwellers and providing them with social services—from child care to vocational training.

The main benefits of systems engineering are probably several years off. What mainly has to be done for urban Negroes right now concerns jobs. Many large corporations eliminated discrimination in hiring years ago. In more recent years, many of them have gone further and actively recruited eligible Negroes. After the riots of 1967, it became clear to many businessmen that even this wasn't enough—that it was also important to hire and train *in*eligible Negro workers. This effort at "reclaiming human resources" has taken several different forms: at some companies nothing more is involved than a businesslike effort to latch onto enough workers in a period of labor scarcity. Some other companies, sensing a large new business opportunity in job training, have gone into the business on a contract basis—e.g., bidding for Job Corps contracts. Finally, a sizable number of companies have plainly staked out positions in job training that are in the nature of "public service." Any profits from these operations will be remote and minimal; in some cases, losses will surely be incurred —more or less deliberately.

These public-service operations are an extraordinary new phenomenon in U.S. business; they are also a principal source of the puzzlement so many businessmen now feel about the extent of their—and their companies'—new involvement in the crisis. In principle, of course, the main objective at most companies is generating profits; "profit maximization" is presumed to be what business is all about.

Not everyone agrees that this *should* be what business is all about; and most businessmen can name some companies at which sales volume seems in fact to be more intensely sought after than profits. But still, the prevailing view of the case is that businessmen who don't try to maximize profits aren't really doing their jobs: if they are employed executives, they are subject to dismissal; if they are corporate directors, they are vulnerable to stockholder suits. Even the barely visible dents in profits represented by corporate charity have been assailed by some stockholders. What, then, about corporate "contributions" that take the form of relatively expensive efforts to recruit, train, and hire uneducated slum Negroes? Or about mortgage investments in the slums that yield appreciably less than alternative investments (which are safer besides)? How far can profit-oriented corporations go with such ventures?

The conventional answer to such questions, volunteered many times by public-spirited businessmen, is that in the long run their inclination to perform good works will also serve to maximize their profits—that, in fact, the profits won't be there unless society is sustained by the kind of good works in question. It is an appealing answer and there is a temptation to swallow it whole; the world would indeed be a wonderful place if profits and good works were so neatly laced together. Unfortunately, however, good works are related more easily to costs than to profits, and where there really is a long-term payoff it will presumably benefit not only the corporation that originally shelled out for those good works, but other corporations too, including competitors that poured all *their* resources into mere profit maximization.

What it comes down to is this: the public and many government officials at various levels have now eagerly embraced the idea that private corporations have a unique capability for dealing with the cities' problems. But many in government, and indeed many businessmen, have not yet perceived that we need new institutional arrangements to help corporations use that capability as well as they might. It will not do to pretend that we can create all the jobs and houses we need simply by appealing to the profit motive. Nor will it do to pretend that corporations can make major investments in the cities on a nonprofit basis.

What kinds of arrangements are called for? Several possibilities come to mind. In some cases, presumably, tax incentives and subsidies might be appropriate when there is no other way to get major corporate involvement. Another possibility would be to allow competitors to form industry councils, with immunity from antitrust action, so that all could engage in "public service" operations from the same competitive base. Some kind of immunity from stockholder action might also be considered. Corporations, and their individual officers and directors, should be freed from concern that any special efforts they put forth will entangle them in court with stockholders. We need a great many more working relationships between our executives, our local planners and government officials, and our universities. In fact, we might well try to evolve a concept of our top managers as a major unused national resource —a resource from which society might expect a lot more. The possibility of a management "tithe" for public service is an intriguing one.

If we really are looking to business to provide some leadership in the cities, what may be needed most of all is a change that will require no new laws, but simply some new attitudes. It is a change already taking place in a good many business communities; its main symptom is a suddenly intense feeling of *involvement* with the city on the part of businessmen. It is this sense of involvement that sent James Roche, the new chairman of General Motors, on a pilgrimage to Lansing to lobby for open housing; and got Henry Ford II to go calling personally on a Negro activist in the Detroit slums. Large and beneficial consequences can be expected as more and more business leaders act on the idea that the city is not just a place where one works and, possibly, lives—but is the major component of America.

Charts on pages 78 through 85 by FORTUNE Art Department and Maurice Berson

✗

PRODUCTION STAFF FOR TIME INCORPORATED
John L. Hallenbeck (Vice President and Director of Production),
Robert E. Foy and Caroline Ferri
Text photocomposed under the direction of Albert J. Dunn and Arthur J. Dunn